WITH THE
TWENTY-NINTH DIVISION
IN GALLIPOLI

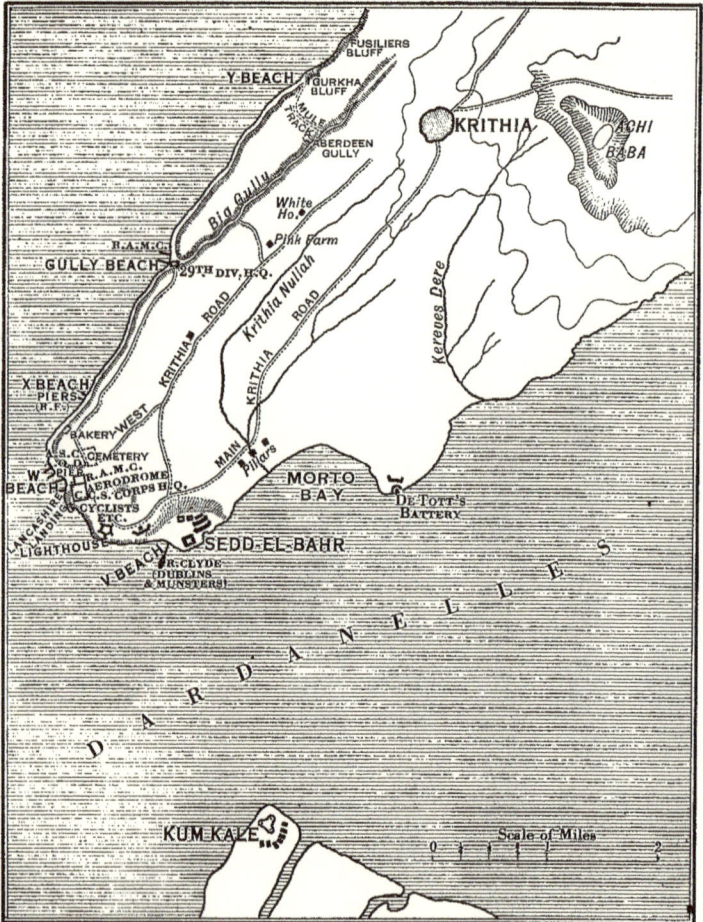

FUSILIERS BLUFF

Y BEACH

GURKHA BLUFF

ABERDEEN GULLY

KRITHIA

ACHI BABA

MULE TRENCH

Big Gully

White Ho.

Pink Farm

R.A.M.C.

GULLY BEACH

29TH DIV. H.Q.

KRITHIA ROAD

KRITHIA NULLAH

KRITHIA ROAD

Kereves Dere

X BEACH PIERS (H.F.)

BAKERY WEST

R.C. CEMETERY

R.A.M.C.

AERODROME

CORPS H.Q.

CYCLISTS ETC.

W BEACH

LANDING PILE

LANCASHIRE LANDING

LIGHTHOUSE

V BEACH

R. CLYDE (DUBLINS & MUNSTERS)

SEDD-EL-BAHR

MAIN

Pillars

MORTO BAY

De Tott's Battery

DARDANELLES

KUM KALE

Scale of Miles

0   1   2

GEORGE PHILIP & SON, LTD.

Longmans, Green & Co., London, New York, Bombay, Calcutta & Madras.

H.M.S. 'IMPLACABLE' FIRING, WITH 2ND ROYAL FUSILIERS IN BOATS, TOWED BY PINNACES MAKING FOR LANDING ON "X" BEACH

This photo must be almost unique. Taken on a mine-sweeper at dawn on April 25.

WITH THE TWENTY-NINTH DIVISION IN GALLIPOLI

A CHAPLAIN'S EXPERIENCES

BY THE

Rev. O. CREIGHTON, C.F.

Church of England Chaplain to the
86th Brigade

WITH TWENTY-SIX ILLUSTRATIONS
AND TWO MAPS

LONGMANS, GREEN AND CO.
39 PATERNOSTER ROW, LONDON
FOURTH AVENUE & 30TH STREET, NEW YORK
BOMBAY, CALCUTTA, AND MADRAS
1916

To the Memory
of many new-found Friends,
whose bodies lie on the Gallipoli Peninsula,
but the fruits of whose devotion
and sacrifice are ours,
and in honour of every officer and man
of the Twenty-ninth Division,
these pages are offered

FOREWORD

At a time when so many books are being written on the war, it is with a feeling of great hesitation that I have decided to add to their number. It was only on returning home for a month's sick leave, after the evacuation of the Gallipoli Peninsula had been completed and one distinct chapter of the war had been finally closed, that, in the press of all that is and will be happening elsewhere, there seemed a danger of the wonderful exploits of the Division which played so leading a part in the Eastern Campaign being forgotten. We had had to abandon the Peninsula. But this does not mean we must forget those who played so heroic a part in this desperate undertaking. Their graves lie in the hands of our enemies, but their memories and examples are ours.

I had been in the somewhat exceptional position of being able to keep a diary throughout the six months that it was my great privilege to be with the 29th Division, and to see different aspects of its life and work from those visible to the ordinary war correspondent or military historian. I am a civilian, and know nothing of military matters beyond what any average civilian may pick up in a campaign. Accordingly, the picture I give is almost solely a human one. Naturally, being in the position of Church of England Chaplain to the 86th Brigade, my diary is very full of allusions, often of a personal nature, to my own special work. And while the diary is published as a memorial to the 29th Division, it would be very difficult to avoid all mention of my work, or my impressions as Chaplain, without destroying the symmetry of the whole.

In war time, as every one knows, the air is full of rumours, and statements made with the most positive certainty are full of inaccuracies. Knowing this, in keeping my diary I took pains to write only what I got at first hand and from personal observation (unless otherwise stated), and in all statements of numbers, etc., tried to be as accurate as possible. Hence the diary is very incomplete. It is no history of the doings of the 29th Division. The regiments I saw most of naturally figure the largest for this reason only, and not because their deeds were more worthy of mention than those of other regiments. I simply give my diary almost in full as it was written, only omitting what would not be of general interest, or personal comments which it would hardly be right or wise to publish. If worth printing at all, the diary must stand on its own merits. I have added some notes here and there, amplifying the text a little, from first-hand information I have since gathered. The photographs have been lent me by Lt. Colonel Newenham, of the 2nd Battalion of the Royal Fusiliers, with which regiment, together with the 1st Battalion of the Lancashire Fusiliers, circumstances brought me most in contact. I wish time had allowed me to collect others illustrating other regiments.

I am greatly indebted to Lt. Colonel Newenham of the Royal Fusiliers, and Major Farmar, formerly of the 86th Brigade Staff, for the valuable accounts of the landings on "X" and "Y" beaches, and the subsequent operations, they have sent me.

I can only feel how inadequate the whole account is. So much more might be said which time and opportunity make it impossible to say. Some may appear to have been signalled out for special mention, while many others, whose deeds are equally worthy of record, are passed by with barely recognition. The limitations under which a diary kept in the midst of such rapidly occurring events must labour, must be the excuse.

I can only hope that the relations and friends of those who took part in the campaign and who fell on the Peninsula, whether recorded or not, will feel that something, however little, has been done to their memory.

February 16, 1916.

CONTENTS

CONTENTS

LIST OF ILLUSTRATIONS

WITH THE TWENTY-NINTH DIVISION IN GALLIPOLI

CHAPTER I

IN ENGLAND

(January 27—March 14)

Leamington Spa: January 27, 1915.—I reached Leamington, the headquarters of the 29th Division, where I had been directed by the War Office to report myself without delay, prepared to go immediately to the front, on the evening of January 27. It was a great wrench tearing myself away from a brigade of the New Army, to which I had been attached shortly after my return from four years' uninterrupted work in the north-west of Canada. I had dropped, quite naturally, into my place in the New Army. Among the officers there were men preparing for Ordination, men I had been at school and college with, and the military life was no stranger for me than for them. I had formed many close friends, and was much interested in my work.

I was presiding at a crowded concert when the telegram from the War Office was suddenly handed to me. I had been looking forward much to going to France with the regiment. Without comment, but with inward feelings of dismay, I handed the telegram to

Captain ——, who was sitting beside me. Many nice things were said at the conclusion, which made it all the harder for me to leave. What was this 29th Division? Regulars just returned from India! I knew nothing about the regular army. I had no soldier friends. What would they be like? I felt I should be like a fish out of water, and it was with fear and trepidation that I presented myself at the Divisional Headquarters, on the evening of the 27th, in the big hotel at Leamington. I met C——, who was to be one of my fellow-chaplains, and who happened to arrive at the same moment at the hotel entrance. We were received by Colonel Percival, who had recently returned from France to be chief of the Divisional Staff.

[*Commencement of diary, which in this chapter has been largely abbreviated as not of general interest.*]

The War Office had not let him know we were coming. However, we produced our papers, and he took us into the office and gave us our railway vouchers. (It is surprising the amount of attention to petty little details these superior officers seem to have to give.) He also gave us lists of all the units composing the Division. From these it appeared that one Brigade was at Rugby, another at Nuneaton, and the third had not been formed yet, but would have its headquarters at Stratford-on-Avon. C—— had an aunt at Rugby, so decided to go there, while I was to go to Nuneaton, leaving the unformed brigade to the chaplain who had not yet arrived. We went to the Regent Hotel for the night. It was the headquarters for the artillery, and swarmed with officers. There were eight batteries there. The whole Division is from India, the last regular Division, I gather, in England.

I understand some units—R.A.M.C., cavalry, A.S.C.,
etc.—are Territorial. We dined at the hotel, and
C—— went off to see a friend, while I wrote letters
and felt a little bored.

Thursday, January 28.—After breakfast I managed
to get into conversation with one or two officers and
gather a little information. The artillery are fully
equipped, but waiting for ammunition. They seemed
a splendid set of men. . . . I went to headquarters
to see if the Communion sets sent by the Chaplain-
General had arrived, and found them there. We saw
the staff officers, who filled in our papers, and then to
lunch at a restaurant, as the hotel was so expensive;
then to the train, where I first saw C—— off to Rugby,
going to Nuneaton myself, and arriving shortly after
4 p.m.

Nuneaton.—I found my way with some difficulty
to the Brigade office, which is some way from the
station, in a large country house, Caldwell Hall, on
the edge of the town. I found a charming Brigade-
Major, Frankland, who had been informed of my
coming from Leamington, had most kindly telephoned
to the vicar to ask if he could have me to stay, and
seemed prepared to do anything, but very busy. I
afterwards discovered he had been in France since the
beginning of the war, but had been recalled to help
form the Division.

The people here have been most active about
soldiers' clubs. They had called in the ubiquitous
Y.M.C.A., and had three clubs started. The main
one is in the Conservative Club, St. George's Hall, a
magnificent room with a stage, in the centre of the
town, with a typical Y.M.C.A. man in charge. He
took me round to see two other clubs. They are not
very much used, as the men are pretty comfortably

billeted, and, having been away from England so long, appreciate a little home life very much.

Friday, January 29.—I went and saw the Brigade-Major, who had very kindly telephoned the night before to the vicar to ask about me, and learnt more about the composition of the 86th Brigade and my duties. In Nuneaton there are three battalions—the 1st Lancashire Fusiliers, the 1st Royal Dublin Fusiliers, and the 2nd Royal Fusiliers—billeted in Stockingford, a mining district just outside. The 1st Royal Munster Fusiliers are at Coventry. The Dublins and Munsters are mainly R.C., but no chaplain seems to have been appointed yet. The L.F.'s and R.F.'s have the usual large majority of nominal C. of E. I am supposed to be attached to the 89th Field Ambulance, but as it is mainly composed of Scotch Presbyterians, I asked the Brigade-Major if I could not be attached to one of the battalions, and I hope this can be managed. Then I went to the L.F.'s orderly-room and found a charming adjutant, who seemed prepared to do anything for me, and also to the Dublins (who have about 120 C. of E.), to arrange about Church Parade. . . . Later, I went to a concert in the St. George's Hall. The battalions all have their bands, but unfortunately the instruments are going away next week, as they do not have bands at the front. The L.F.'s band was playing cheery but noisy music. They are to play at church on Sunday. A very nice, rather talkative corporal accosted me in a shop afterwards, and asked if I was to be their chaplain. He gave me a lot of useful information. He said the men were not at all religious, and I would have a lot of disappointments, but would always find them very civil. They did not like going to church. They had a splendid chaplain in India—a soldiers' chaplain, quite unlike the English ones. He seemed quite prepared to instruct me, and very pleased that I was prepared to let him.

These are some of my first impressions. Regulars are very different from Kitchener's Army. They seem exceedingly smart and seasoned troops, and have an air that there is nothing they don't know about soldiering. Of course one feels that they have inherited an ancient army tradition, and there is not the feeling of new ground to be broken there was with Kitchener's Army. It makes so much difference, feeling they are so absolutely ready for the front. I found people friendly before, but nothing could exceed the friendliness here. There seems nothing they are not prepared to do. I can see how my work will be both easier and harder. It will run much more smoothly, but there will be a great barrier of tradition and forms to surmount. The men seem to be very well behaved, but of course in a town of this size there must be much that is wrong. I can only say how thankful I am that I do not come to them utterly green. I do know a little military terminology now, and understand a little my way about. It is all exceedingly interesting. I don't think I shall aim at much during our weeks here beyond trying to make friends with as many officers and men as possible. I think there will be more chance of ancient traditions breaking down when we go out.

Saturday, January 30.—I spent the morning on a route march with the L.F.'s. I went to the parade ground, when the Major came and spoke to me; and when they moved off, and I fell to the rear, he sent for me to come and march beside him at the head of the battalion, just behind the band, and there I marched all the way. We had a little guard of soldiers round

us to keep the crowd off. Different companies took
it in turn to take the lead, so I had an opportunity of
talking to different officers. They were all most
friendly and agreeable. The Major was especially
nice. He told me that the 1st L.F.'s have not seen
service since the Crimea, and are all very keen to get
out. They have been a very long time in India.
They feel the cold rather, but are getting acclimatized.
A huge band of about seventy instruments went before
us, and I enjoyed the music much more out of doors.
It certainly makes a difference to marching. I tried
my new patent boots, and found them on the whole
very satisfactory. The officers took much interest in
them. I talked a little with the regimental sergeant-
major. He had been to Aldershot to see his wife, and
had seen the review of Kitchener's Army when the
French Minister was there, and was very much impressed by the men. I was pleased to hear this, as
I could not help contrasting the regulars with the
Kitcheners, unfavourably to the latter. These are
splendid troops here, such a magnificent physique.
I enjoyed the march much, and hope to go for more.

Sunday, January 31.—After breakfast a motor-car
came for me and took me to the Stockingford Church,
where the R.F.'s were parading at ten o'clock. It
was my first military parade with regulars. The band
provided the music, and also the choir. The whole
service was done with the most exact precision. A
Major read the lessons. One felt they had been doing
it for years, just the same. The vicar took the service.
I asked that no ladies should be present. However,
I saw some girls in the gallery with the soldiers.
Fortunately, they were ejected before the sermon. I
only preached for seven minutes. I told the men I
knew little about them and the place, and had only

heard good. But I said that the women and girls were having a very difficult time during the war. They had never had military in the place before, and were naturally very excited, and thought a lot of the soldiers who had just come from India and were going so soon to the front. I asked the men to do all they could to help the girls, so that the memory they left behind them should always be of the good they had done during their stay.

But I am afraid the men do not like Church Parade. Very few go to Evensong, and I have not heard of one going to a Celebration. Theirs is a strange religion. I held a service in the evening in the St. George's Hall. There were very few men there, mostly R.C., I think, and they did not sing the hymns, and seemed very loath to stand, and I had to realise they were very different from Kitchener's Army. Individually, I must say I find them very nice, very civil and easy to talk to. But I feel quite at sea as to how to do any direct religious work with them, and almost inclined not to attempt any, but just to try and get to know them.

Monday, February 1.—I went a long route march with the Dublins in the morning, about twelve miles. The Colonel rode part of the way, but walked a good deal, and was very pleasant, and talked away quite a lot. Many of the officers are very pleasant, but I don't feel they very much care whether one exists or not. After all, why should they? Again I marched just behind the band, and enjoyed the music. It is very amusing watching whole villages turn out to see us and the general excitement we arouse.

Tuesday, February 2.—Mrs. —— told me she had heard stories of soldiers leaving their billets at late hours to meet girls in back streets, so I decided to investigate a little on my own. . . . At 10.30 p.m. I went for an hour's walk along a path by the canal. It was a lovely moonlight night, but I saw no one there, and found a few soldiers behaving quite orderly in the streets, in one or two cases with girls, but quite openly. I find they are allowed out till midnight. One of the other vicars has since told me that he has been out three nights, but saw nothing. I am very glad, as now I feel able to contradict a lot of the reports going about. The men seem to be behaving very well.

Thursday, February 4.— . . . After lunch I bicycled to Stockingford and saw the Adjutant of the R.F.'s, and went round with him a little, and then bicycled on to Arbury Park, a large place, where one of the companies was trench-digging. The R.F.'s are all Cockneys, mostly from the East End of London— such a contrast to the L.F.'s. They are smaller men, but seem very tough. They never stop talking and joking. It might pall in peace-time, but I think would be very suitable to the trenches. They were digging in awful mud, and bailing the water out of the trenches with pails. They all seem very comfortable in their billets, and the soldiers' club is being closed up there, as it is not used. This billeting makes it exceedingly difficult to see the men or do anything with them.

Friday, February 5.—Went to Coventry. One of my battalions, the Munsters, is there. I went to the orderly-room and found they had over 200 Anglicans, but had not yet been to Church Parade, and the Adjutant asked me to arrange one. . . . The South Wales Borderers are also there, and, though not in my brigade, I went to arrange a parade for them. They are back from Tsing-Tau, where they were for eleven days in terribly muddy trenches, but only lost fourteen men, and have brought back practically all their wounded, who have recovered. . . .

Saturday, February 6.—I went to the 89th Field Ambulance headquarters and found a very nice Colonel, and arranged about my being attached to them. They are all Presbyterian. I gathered a R.C. padre had been appointed.

Sunday, February 7.— . . . I had supper with Dr. ——. He told me there had been thirty soldiers married at the registrar's office. However, when we inquired we found there had only been nine licences issued; most of the men being married at the R.C. Church. Things do get so exaggerated.

Monday, February 8.— . . . I went to the club and talked to the men. They are so nice to talk to. C—— finds just as I do, that practically none go to Communion. I am trying to discover if there are any C.E.M.S. men, or men belonging to any religious society, but hitherto have been unsuccessful. They all seem to have had any individuality crushed out of them by army discipline. They confess this, and say themselves that it is useless ever calling for volunteers to do anything. They must always be detailed. I am trying to get up a concert, and the men have to be detailed in regimental orders in order to come to rehearsals. They don't mind being detailed, but won't come unless they are.[1] But they are charming men, so civil and clean and orderly. I don't think I have heard an oath yet, and others say the same. I hear nothing definite about our departure yet, and they seem quite leisurely about completing equipment.

Thursday, February 11.—A dull day. The main excitement was that I heard over the telephone from

[1] These remarks express a somewhat crude first impression, largely modified by subsequent experience.

the R.A.M.C. sergeant-major that my batman had arrived. I had to explain that, as I was from Kitchener's army, I did not know what a batman was. Perhaps he could send it over by an orderly. It turned out it was my servant, sent specially from the A.S.C., from the other end of England somewhere, to look after me. I am glad the Government takes such care of the chaplains.

Friday, February 12.—This morning I went on a great brigade route march. The whole brigade turned out, with all their transport. It was a lovely day, and a fine sight. We went fourteen miles, and did not get back till three o'clock. The Munsters joined us from Coventry for part of the way. I timed the whole column as it passed a certain point, and it took twenty-five minutes. I talked to different officers on the way, and found them all very pleasant.

Tuesday, February 16.—I went to a dinner party given to the senior Dublin officers by Mr. T——, a wealthy mill-owner on whom the Colonel is billeted. The General and Brigade-Major and about sixteen Dublin officers were there. The General was previously in command of a territorial brigade, but is very pleased to be here, and enthusiastic about the men. We had much to eat and drink, and toasts at the end. I was made to sit in the place of honour at the head of the table. They were all very charming to me. Certainly the regular officer is very easy to get on with. They started a great discussion at my end of the table about compulsory Church Parade. I was very glad to find the majority strongly in favour of its being voluntary, and firmly convinced that if only the men liked the padre they would come. The Colonel made me play auction bridge afterwards, and they were very nice when I rather demurred about playing for money, and let me off. It was a very pleasant evening, and a good way to get to know the officers.

Wednesday, February 17.— . . . Father Finn, the R.C. chaplain, came to see me and seemed very pleasant.

I went to a room where the L.F.'s have lectures for the men. The officer who was to lecture had so bad a cold that he said he could not. So I offered to tell them about the Canadian contingent, and he jumped at it. The Lancashire men are very quiet, and sat perfectly stolid while I tried to tell them why it was so difficult to get the kind of discipline among Canadians the English regulars are used to. We know nothing of our movements yet.

Thursday, February 25.—The Divisional General suddenly decided to have an inspection. The orders had to be given out as late as 1 a.m. that morning, and the bugle roused the majority (but not me) at 5 a.m. I rode out after them, and got to the saluting-base as our brigade passed. The 87th Brigade from Rugby was out too, but I did not see them. So was the Field Ambulance, for the first time, and I took my right place on the column with the Colonel. The Divisional General is Major-General Shaw.[1] He was a Brigadier at the beginning of the war, but he was wounded, and has been laid up some weeks since Christmas. The Brigadier is General Hare. His staff say it is a privilege to work with him, and the Colonels speak highly of him. So we are very fortunate. In the evening I went to rather a poor concert in the hall. I had secured the R.F.'s band for the next evening, but had no singers. So I went off to a local music-hall whose manager had promised to help me if I wished,

[1] On the day of the royal inspection Major-General Shaw handed over the Division to Major-General Hunter-Weston.

and he took me round behind the scenes, where I interviewed a coy and buxom woman who sang patriotic songs, in her dressing-room, and a blind man who played the concertina, and they both promised to come round and help between their turns.

Friday, February 26.—I went to a piece of ground where the L.F.'s were digging trenches, and the Colonel carried me off while he distributed sixty-four beautiful wrist-watches to the men who had made the best scores shooting, and then to inspect the transport and horses and the wonderful travelling kitchens which cook meals on the march, and the water-carts which have a filtering arrangement attached which makes it possible to use any water. In the evening came my concert. The R.F.'s band played beautifully, and the lady from the music-hall made a tremendous hit with patriotic songs. She had no voice, but boundless cheek, and made the men sing choruses, and finally made a touching little speech wishing them the best of luck. The blind man also had a great reception, and played the concertina beautifully, and it was quite one of our most successful concerts.

Monday, March 1.—In the afternoon I rode off to join the R.F.'s, who were going out for the night. When I joined them the Colonel told me they were going to billet in a neighbouring village, and said I could come, and the Adjutant said he had a billet for me. So I tore back for some kit, and soon rejoined them. We went to Wolvey, a little village of 600 people, five miles out. We were greeted on arrival by the church bells pealing. I was billeted with two other officers in the vicarage, and slept on a sofa. I attended a conference of officers in the evening, which was very interesting. The General came out to see the billeting, and I had a nice talk with him. The men were put in schools and barns and empty houses, 650 in all. I looked into the schools after they had gone to bed, and could not see the floor for men. The windows were all shut, and they were mostly smoking, so you may imagine the state of the atmosphere. However, they were very happy. Next morning, at 8.15, as many as possible packed into the church, and we had a delightful little service taken by the vicar. Then we went off on outpost duty, and while I was waiting about the Colonel sent for me, and we had a lovely ride all round the country inspecting the outposts. I walked most of the way back, and this time made friends with a number of the men. They are very easy to get on with, and are always cheery and laughing. If they pass me on the march now they usually call out good-morning or good-afternoon, and this afternoon I heard one say, "Now then all together," followed by a chorus of "Good day, sir."

We are now fully equipped and ready to start, and may be called up any moment. However, nothing is known.

Coventry: Saturday, March 6.—After many orders and counter-orders we were told the brigade was to move to Coventry. I rode off with pack and haver-sack, saddle-bags and pouches, in full marching order. I joined the headquarters transport, and rode with a staff-officer and the veterinary surgeon all along the tram-lines. The transport horses were very lively. I was again billeted on the vicar, where I was exceed-ingly comfortable. Captain and Mrs. F—— are here. He is staff-captain.

Sunday, March 7.—My servant at last turned up. He had been thoroughly incompetent, and had lost my luggage in the transport, and seemed quite incapable of tackling a new situation. I took a delightful parade service in the magnificent St. Michael's Church, nearly all the R.F.'s and their officers being present, and also some of the Munsters. Afterwards I went to the brigade office and saw F——, who told me orders had arrived practically pointing to our going to the Dardanelles. Every one is to be measured for helmets, and heavy draught horses are to be handed in.

Monday, March 8.—I went up to London to see the Chaplain-General and get books for the Dardanelles. I also ordered Gospels from the Scripture Gift Office. I stopped off at Rugby on the way back and saw C——, and discussed the new move. I do hope it is the Dardanelles. It is about time we went somewhere.

Thursday, March 11.—We had a big sham battle. Our brigade, with some artillery, went out to attack a skeleton army of cyclists holding a line on the other side of the Avon. I rode out with the R.F.'s. There was the usual waiting about. At last I got away and rode ahead, crossing the Avon and finding myself among the enemy. However, operations ended much sooner than was expected, and we got home about 3 p.m. I heard we were to have an early parade at 7.30 for the whole Division, but purpose and destination were kept entirely secret. However, we all guessed it must mean a Royal Inspection.

Friday, March 12.—I rode off with Captain F—— at 7.30. We joined the R.F.'s, who had started early, after a bit, and I stayed with them most of the rest of the day. We went seven or eight miles, and got on to a fine road with a wide grass border on either side, in which grew a magnificent avenue of elms and oaks. Every side road was blocked by a policeman, but the whole thing had been kept so secret there was practically no one about. At last the order came to halt, and we all drew up in a long line, four deep, on one side of the road under the trees. The whole line must have stretched three or four miles. After a longish wait the men were called to attention, and a little cavalcade of staff-officers came riding down the road through the trees, with the King at their head. I sat on my horse just between the R.F.'s and the Munsters. The Colonel of the R.F.'s was beside me, and, as did all the Colonels, walked down the line of his regiment with the King. The King seemed very much interested. No one had been told officially he was coming. Then, after another long wait, the march past started. Our brigade simply marched past in fours. I rode with the leading regiment of the leading brigade. The King and his staff were at a cross road, some way down. After we had passed I broke off and got among the little crowd that had collected. It was wonderful seeing the long line of silver bayonets winding through the trees like a stream. It seemed quite endless watching 12,000 infantry pass. Unfortunately, I missed the artillery and other divisional troops, as they had passed ahead of us. There must have been 18,000 men altogether. It seemed vast, and the men were magnificent. The King has sent us a very nice little message.

Saturday, March 13.—My servant appeared with a telegram saying his wife was very ill, which had been accepted by the Colonel of the Field Ambulance as a reason for his going home for the night. So I could say nothing, though I felt certain it was a lie, and hardly expected to see him next day. Meanwhile, orders had gone out that we were to leave next day. I received official instructions, marked secret, about all I was to do. I was fortunate in being billeted with the Staff-Captain, who had all arrangements in hand, as he made every provision for my comfort. So I bicycled down to the R.F.'s, to whom I was to be attached for the journey. I had hoped to have Church Parade next morning, but the Colonel and Adjutant, though they would have liked it, asked me not to, as so many of the men would be bicycling back to Nuneaton to see their friends and sweethearts, that they would be left with a tremendous list of absentees to punish on the voyage. I went and bought a box of a hundred books for the journey, for the men, which the Adjutant asked me to get.

Sunday, March 14.—I was called with the news that our departure had been postponed for twenty-four hours.

THE QUAY, ALEXANDRIA, WITH H.M.T. 'A———'

CHAPTER II

ON BOARD SHIP

(*March* 15—27)

March 15.—Exactly a month after the day we were to be ready to leave, I made some final purchases in the town, got packed, and visited orderly rooms in the morning. I decided to go down early to escape a crush, and travelled with the Brigade Headquarters Staff and the A.S.C., leaving at 2.40. Many farewells, though our departure at the station was very quiet, as the men had not had time to make friends at Coventry. What a mercy it is to be a bachelor on these occasions! We had a very uneventful journey down, reaching Avonmouth at 6.40. The rest were going on different boats, so I made my own way to the *A*——, which was to take my own two special regiments, the R.F.'s and the L.F.'s. I was the first to arrive, and dined with two embarkation Majors. They said they had already embarked the Naval Division, who are presumably now at the Dardanelles. They had also disembarked recently 3500 Canadians and some Australians, all of whom, they said, had been some of the finest men they had ever handled, and so well disciplined. This boat had had its last trip from New York. I got to my cabin, very large and comfortable, and waited for the first train, which arrived about 12.30 a.m., and watched them go on board. I eventually turned in about 2.30, and slept undisturbed, though they kept arriving all night. I am the only chaplain on board, with two whole battalions and a company of the Munsters. She is a second-class boat, but very spacious and comfortable, and we have plenty of room.

Tuesday, March 16.—Well, they continued to arrive all the morning, and I decided to slip away and go to Bristol to buy a few more things. It is terrible how one goes on buying and thinking of more things. I found the Colonel of the Dublins buying things. He said his servant had left all his kit behind on the platform, and he had to get an entirely new outfit. I found every one had arrived on my return, and they were wearing life-belts and being shown where to stand in case of being torpedoed. After lunch I wandered off to the ship on which the rest of the Brigade and the General and Staff were travelling. It is a very small, uncomfortable boat, and they were very crowded, four officers in a tiny cabin and a miserable little dining-room. I asked the General why he did not come with the Staff to our boat, and he said he did not like to change now they were actually starting on active service. It would hardly look well.

When I got back I found the Depôt chaplain waiting for me. The Chaplain-General had telegraphed to him to see the Division off, and see if we were properly supplied with books, etc. We had tea with the General and Brigade-Major, who had come over to visit us. I then rushed off with the chaplain to see the boat which was taking all the transport and various oddments, and another taking the artillery. I found such a nice C.O., who said he was so sorry there was no chaplain on board, but would be glad of books and would take services himself.

Then I rushed back to my boat, which was hooting

preparatory to departure. Four tugs came and towed us out of the harbour through the lock, and we could see an escort of three destroyers steaming up and signalling. The Colonel ordered another life-belt parade, and we were slowly towed through the lock wearing these ridiculous-looking things. It had been a lovely afternoon, perfectly calm. Everything was quite quiet as we went out. In the lock the chaplain threw a lot of little pamphlets from the Chaplain-General on board for the men. Then we all went down to supper, where I sat at a table with the L.F.'s officers. Nearly every one went to bed pretty early as they had all been up the night before.

We were all expecting to anchor outside and wait for the other boats to load up, but to our surprise we did not stop. We were on the first boat of the whole Division to leave. Very strict orders were given. No lights were allowed. We had to sleep in our clothes with life-belts at hand. At 10.30 I went on deck. It was very dark. The boat was steaming ahead in perfect darkness and silence. I could just dimly make out the form of a destroyer accompanying us with no lights. It was very mysterious. It was very uncomfortable sleeping in my clothes. The officer sharing my cabin had to go on guard at midnight. We heard afterwards that a submarine had been sighted by one of the destroyers. And still no transport has been sunk as yet, and the Navy carries on the constant transport of men and munitions through all the submarines. The absolute secrecy and stealthiness of it all is wonderful.

Wednesday, March 17.—We woke to an absolutely calm morning and no destroyers. Our only protection now lies in the machine-guns which have been mounted at different points. Time passes quickly.

We all have drill with life-belts. This afternoon I was vaccinated, talked to the men, saw about distributing books, and arranged about holding voluntary meetings for the two regiments during the evenings. This will be quite an experiment.

Thursday to Monday, March 18 *to* 22—Nothing much is gained by keeping a chronological record of a voyage, as each day is much the same. The weather has been perfect, absolutely calm, warm but fresh. The boat is exceedingly comfortable without being luxurious (it is a second-class boat). The food is quite good and plentiful. There is plenty of room in cabins, saloons and on the decks. Life on a troopship is wonderfully orderly and smooth. Everything follows a carefully arranged programme. I usually am up by 7. 15, when the officers of one regiment do physical drill and I join them. It made me most frightfully stiff for a while, but I am getting over it now. Then there are rounds at 10.30, when the Colonels inspect their battalions and the Captain goes round his ship, followed by drill and probably a lecture for the officers, which I sometimes attend. In the afternoon, boat drill and all kinds of inspection of kit and issuing various things, and occasionally examinations for the officers. In fact the day goes very quickly. Supper at 7 p.m., and then I begin, first going to one regiment at 7.30 and then another at 8.15 to 9. I was quite amazed at the way the men responded and the crowds that came. They love singing hymns, and I discourse to them about all kinds of things, telling them a little Turkish history sometimes. I am practically always followed by X——, a very genuine man and simply overflowing with zeal. He does not mind what he says or who he says it to. He told his Colonel that if any ticklish job had to be done he had better choose him, as he was perfectly ready and none of the others were.

The Colonel is an exceedingly strict and devout R. C. He is a most charming and interesting man, and his whole regiment thinks very highly of him. He is well read and extremely unassuming, and delightful to talk to. Very strict on parade. Frightfully keen on his work, especially the managing of men. Foremost among the admirers is X——, despite the fact that the Colonel is an R.C. But X—— discovered that he sent a subscription to the Salvation Army on leaving India, and this impressed him tremendously. I don't think he cares much for the Church. One of the regimental doctors is much perturbed about the Church, finds it perfectly dead and dogmatic and disunited. So there is much talk. I cannot say that the Church seems to raise much enthusiasm among the officers.

The men are really just like so many children. They have been writing reams of mawkish sentimental letters to the Nuneaton girls, which the officers have had to censor. I don't know of a single man who thought of buying a book or magazine for the journey. And now they hang round when not drilling, longing for something to read. Fortunately, I bought some books before leaving, but they have not gone round far. They behave extremely well, give no trouble, and are perfectly docile. You very rarely hear them slanged by either officers or N.C.O.'s. They take everything for granted as it comes along, grumbling a little and longing to be back with Susy or May in Nuneaton. They are always very friendly and responsive.

The tone among the officers seems very high, and they strike me as a nice, clean-living, straightforward, moderate lot of men. One or two are quite intelligent and have interests outside the army, but the younger ones are mostly interested in sport, etc. None of them put the least bit of side on, and they all work hard at their jobs and have a strong sense of responsibility.

On Sunday I had a Celebration, four parade services, and a voluntary evening service. Every weekday I have two voluntary services for the men and one for the officers. I also visit the men in hospital.

Tuesday, March 23.—At noon we arrived at Malta after a very quick voyage of six and a half days. A French destroyer was protecting the entrance to the harbour, and an examination boat came to ask us who we were and whither bound. After a good deal of signalling to the shore and waiting we were allowed to go into the harbour and moor. Valetta is a wonderfully picturesque place, and the harbour is very interesting, landlocked on all sides, with houses clustering on hills and rocks all round. Valetta has all been built of stone quarried from the rock on which it stands, and is capped with massive fortifications of the old Knights of Malta. There are many huge buildings and everything is solid. It suggested many sketches. Crowds of boats put out from shore and sold things to the soldiers. I was the first to go ashore, thinking our stay would be short. I went to three Soldiers' Homes and collected bundles of literature for the men, and then to the Junior A. and N. Stores to buy one or two things. The town is most interesting. The flocks of goats are very quaint. The streets are extremely narrow. The women wear a quaint head-dress rather like a large black nun's veil caught up on one side. I believe it was ordered by the Pope as a penance for their conduct with the French soldiers when Napoleon took Malta.[1] The whole place is dominated by

[1] Subsequent inquiry makes it probable that this is not the correct explanation.

the Church, which is very powerful. I went over the Cathedral, which is supposed to be very fine, but too gaudy for me. Some of the courtyards with trees growing up from the paved courts are very picturesque. I had tea in a shop and then returned to the boat for dinner, to find we were going to spend the night there. So practically all the officers went to the opera. It was a special performance of *Faust*. I went with six others in a large central box just under the box of the Governor, Lord Methuen, who was there. Faust and Mephistopheles were very good, and so was the orchestra, but chorus bad. However, I enjoyed it. Afterwards we went to the Club, a mighty palace of the Knights, had supper and got back at 1.30.

Wednesday, March 24.—Our departure was again postponed. Several other transports arrived. I spent most of the day with one of the doctors exploring the town, and we poked about and saw many interesting things. The guard-room opposite the governor's palace is all covered with pictures painted on the walls by different officers who have been on guard throughout the English occupation, and is rather amusing. We went over fortifications, into various churches, one of which is all decorated with bones and skulls, saw the old hospital with a huge ward five hundred feet long, which is being got ready, and various other places. We lunched at the club and had tea in a shop, and got back to the boat for dinner.

I have not written my diary for ages. However, I must try and make up now.

Thursday, March 25.—We left Malta early, about 7 a.m., and were out of sight of land all day.

Friday, March 26.—In the afternoon sighted south of Greece, and had an exciting time at sunset as we rounded the southern cape, Malea, going between it and the little island of Cerigo. Just as it was getting dusk we suddenly sighted the French navy right behind a little island. Two destroyers came out to have a look at us and cheered very heartily. Our men are very slow to answer cheers and usually look on gaping. Then we all went down to supper, and of course every one was asking how it was the French navy was allowed to shelter in a Greek bay. We were going very slowly and would be passing through islands all night. It was a lovely night. Of course we were all very much wondering where we were going and what was going to happen. The ship was to be guarded the whole night by men all round the decks, who were to be on the look-out, as far as we could understand, for friendly French submarines. There was to be absolute silence. At ten o'clock I went out on deck, to be met by an officer who said: "Do you know we have just turned right round and are going back the way we came?" The ship was also going very much faster. Then a wireless message arrived for the Colonel, and of course we were all guessing and wondering what it all meant when we heard we were to go to Alexandria at once. More guessing. I felt sure there must be trouble in Egypt. There was every possible suggestion made.

We coasted along the northern shore of Crete, always lovely weather.

Saturday, March 27.—Made across open sea to Alexandria.

CHAPTER III

IN EGYPT

(*March* 28—*April* 8)

Sunday, March 28 (*Palm Sunday*).—Reached Alexandria about 10 a.m. I had a Celebration at 7 a.m. and parade services in morning and afternoon as before, four altogether, and a voluntary service at night. It appeared that Lemnos was an impossible base, no proper harbour, no water, and that things were not ready for a landing. We were to concentrate at Alexandria. I rushed down town with an officer in the late afternoon. Alexandria is a huge place, with a mighty harbour simply full of shipping. There were a number of German prize boats and an American battleship; also many French transports with Zouaves, etc., on board. The town swarmed with soldiers of every possible kind. It was some way to the centre of the town, but we got on a tram and went to a mighty square, with fine buildings all round. I was especially taken with St. Mark's Church, built in a very effective Moorish style and very cool inside.

I leave this as I wrote it. Subsequently we found what a magnificent harbour Mudros (Lemnos island) offered. I believe that there had recently been a violent gale, and that some of the ships had dragged their anchors, which may account for the reports we heard. Considering the difficulty of operations it was an exceedingly suitable place for an intermediate base, as it subsequently became.   Alexandria, of course, was *the* base.   The water difficulty was got over by the ships bringing water, and later by the erection of a plant for distilling water from the sea.

Monday, March 29.—We had one of those tedious days of waiting,[1] which seem so common in the Army. The men all got off the ship and sat on the quay till about four o'clock, doing absolutely nothing.   There seems to have been a good deal of muddle about our coming.   However, we eventually all started off to the camp, about five miles out of town, on a strip of desert between a salt lake and the sea, with salt piles and stone quarries around, at a place called Mex.   The camp was about one and a half miles beyond the tram terminus.   We found our tents, which we had brought with us, already pitched.   I was given one to myself, and so was very comfortable.   I messed with the Headquarters mess of the R.F.'s, *i.e.* the Colonel, the Major, the Adjutant, the machine gun, signalling, and medical officers.   We managed to feed very well.   I slept in my valise on the ground, and got quite used to it after a time.

Tuesday, March 30.—I went in to town in the morning with the doctor and called on the Archdeacon.   I discovered the Bishop was about, and wanted to find out if he would come and hold a Confirmation, also about getting reading matter, etc., for the men.   He took me round to the Soldiers' and Sailors' Institute, kept by Mr. and Mrs. D——.   It was a fine big place. crowded with soldiers of all kinds, who were being sent there for their meals.   They gave me lunch, and

---

[1] I remember a Major saying to me at the time: " I have been twenty-five years in the Army, and reckon that ten of them have been spent in waiting."

THE QUAY AT ALEXANDRIA, WITH KIT BAGS AND AMBULANCE

in the afternoon Mr. D—— came out to Mex with me
to see what we could do. Eventually I decided to
try and get a tent up. Where was the money to come
from? I interviewed the Brigade-Major and he said
it would be quite all right. Well, it all involved a
good deal of running round for the next few days
which is of no particular interest. By Wednesday
night I had a huge native tent up, about 100ft. by 36ft.,
made of a kind of thick canvas, all beautifully decorated inside with coloured *appliqué* work and lit with a
large arc lamp. I borrowed tables and benches from
a building close by. I interviewed all the Colonels,
and got them each day to let me have a transport
wagon in turn, and two men told off from each regiment to run it. For the first two or three days I had
to go in pretty well all day with the sergeant in charge,
and buy stuff, pastries by the hundred dozen, oranges
and cigarettes by the thousand. Buying is not easy
in a strange town and unknown language; but we
managed pretty well. Only they were very slow.
However much we bought it was impossible to keep
pace with the demand. We could not open the canteen till 6 p.m., but everything was gone long before
nine. The men had to be formed up in a long queue
and file in one behind the other, while I had six or
seven men serving as hard as they could go. I fear
we lost money the first day, as there were one or two
men helping I did not know about, but we got a much
better system working later. I got a large supply of
magazines and games, writing-paper, etc. The place
was a seething mass in the evenings. There were
8000 men encamped out there, and not allowed out
of camp. The contractors' canteens were small and
badly managed by Greeks, and there was a lot of
confusion. I had a very good staff to work it. It kept

me extremely busy. Besides all this it was Holy
Week. On Good Friday I managed to go to a nice
quiet little two-hours' service taken by the Bishop in
St. Mark's, and saw him after it, and he promised to
come out one day. We imagined we were probably
going to have a prolonged stay. I had a delightful
service on Good Friday evening, when the tent was
simply packed with a parade of the R.F.'s, the L.F.'s
coming voluntarily. They had had a long tiring day
practising landing from boats. C—— and D——
(chaplains) had also arrived and I saw something of
them. They stick with the Field Ambulance. I have
got attached to the regiment temporarily.

I would like to take this opportunity of expressing
my unbounded admiration for the work done in Alexandria by Mr. and Mrs. D——. I saw a good deal
of them, not only on this occasion, but subsequently,
when I also stayed at the Institute. Men will be found
in every single regiment of the M.E.F. who will bear
out this testimony. Mrs. D—— seemed to me to
exercise exactly that unconscious and motherly in-
fluence over our soldiers, British, Australian, and New
Zealand alike, which means so much to the men when
away from their homes. And it was all done in such
a quiet and unobtrusive way. Mr. D—— was indefatigable in extending their work to outlying camps
surrounding Alexandria. They were both of the
greatest help to me.

Easter Day, April 4.—I had Celebrations at 6.30 and
11 (only about forty communicants altogether) in the
tent which I shared with the R.C., and parade service
in the open, when I preached from a wagon. I had a
delightful voluntary service in the evening in the tent,
which was crammed, officers also coming, and after it,
took the names of those who wished to be confirmed,
forty-six in all, from the different regiments and more

29TH DIVISION CAMP AT MEX, NEAR ALEXANDRIA

later. The majority were from the L.F.'s. I was most surprised to find a large number in proportion from each of the Irish regiments, where there are only a few Anglicans, and very few from the R.F.'s, which is, practically, entirely C. of E. There were three sergeants among them.

Well, the difficulty always is classes. You cannot arrange a time without half the men being employed. However, I settled I would have two classes every day, at 5.30 and 6.30, and that men must come to at least four during the week, and that the Bishop would come the following Sunday. I held classes on Monday and Tuesday and they were splendidly attended, and practically the whole of Tuesday I sat in my tent and saw the men singly, and found them very anxious to change their lives. Sometimes it was a girl they had taken up with in England that had changed them, sometimes our gatherings on board ship, sometimes they had for long been anxious to be confirmed. I found a number had started to say their prayers in the tents. In fact it was a wonderful experience, and the men were all very delightful. C—— had some candidates as well. However, it seemed so likely that we would be off soon that I decided to try and get the Bishop (who was at Cairo) earlier. So I telephoned to the Archdeacon to Tuesday, and it was settled he should be there on Thursday at 6.30. And then on Wednesday we awoke to find we were all off. Most of the regiments left that day. We did not go till Thursday, but it made the Confirmation impossible. However, I was very glad to have made the start and have all the men's names down.

From the point of view of my work as chaplain, our stay at Mex was quite one of my most wonderful experiences. The whole brigade was in camp close together.   I had a huge tent to meet the men in, besides the continual opportunity of going round the tents of officers and men alike.   It was perfect weather, and the men did not have much to do and were not allowed out of camp.   I got to know so many of the men so well individually, and they came to me quite freely. And the officers simply made me feel I was one of them.   I shall never forget the Confirmation Classes. We sat in a circle on the sand just outside the big tent.   The only light was the new moon and an electric torch I had to help me write the men's names down. I was greatly surprised at the regularity with which they came and the quietness with which they listened. It was a great disappointment to them that the Confirmation could not be held.   But, of course, I told them that the blessing was theirs just the same, as they had shown such sincerity, and so true a change in their outlook on life.   I keep meeting the men who came to the classes on the peninsula, and afterwards in hospitals, etc.

I could not have wished for better men than the little staff I collected from the whole brigade to work the canteen, in the big tent, and it meant real hard work.   But they entered into it with zest, and we often spoke of it afterwards.   It is on these occasions that one forms very real and lasting friendships, and barriers are broken down.

And quite as delightful was the intercourse with the officers of the R.F.'s and L.F.'s, of whom I saw most. They all seemed old friends, and treated me, though a stranger and a padre, as one of themselves.   It was an exceedingly happy time and a delightful memory.

And lastly I cannot speak too highly of the help I had from the brigade staff, and the colonels, adjutants, and especially transport officers, in the difficult work of running the big tent.   I had only to ask for men, fatigue parties, transport, etc., and they were at once granted.   I mention this as showing the real interest the authorities showed in their men's comfort.

I find I made no mention in my diary of the inspection held by the Commander-in-Chief of the two brigades camped at Mex. It was a wonderful sight, seeing them all massed together with plenty of room to manœuvre on the stretches of smooth sand. I rode to a little hill at a distance and dismounted as I watched them. My groom had not tightened my saddle-girths, and when I tried to mount again the saddle slipped round and I rolled off. The regiments at the moment were marching off in column. Imagine my dismay as I saw my horse take fright and tear off right past the Commander-in-Chief and his staff, and then all among the men, nearly upsetting the column. It was some little time before he was recaptured.

April 7.—Wednesday I had to spend rushing round the town finishing things up. We made so much money at the tent that from six days' takings we were able to pay all expenses, which were over £20, and have a balance of £10 left.

Thursday, April 8.—We returned to the *A*——, by this time the South Wales Borderers had taken the place of the L.F.'s, for which I was rather sorry, though they seem a very nice lot. The General and his staff are also on board, and among them F——, which is nice. My greatest tragedy hitherto is that I have lost my box of parade books and Testaments, etc. They put it into a wrong truck on the train, and it was taken off with a lot of tents to the ordnance stores. I rushed round the town after it, but it was not to be found. Perhaps it may follow me. I saw H——, the senior chaplain of the Division, just before we left. A kind of chaplain-general to the whole Mediterranean forces had been sent out by the Chaplain-General, Hordern by name, an Anglican, whom I met in Alexandria and who seemed very nice. If I want anything I am to tell H——, and H—— will write to him. His orders are that the chaplains are in no case to go in front of the advance dressing-station. He says they are always anxious to get up to the front, where they can only be of use at one point in the line, and meanwhile men are being brought in to the receiving-station from all along the line. Of course this means that I shall presumable be pretty safe. But I am very much wondering whether I shall be able to watch the others go off and stay behind.

I think there must have been a misunderstanding on this point. At the time there was only one C. of E. chaplain to each brigade, in fact we had only three to the whole Division. The question was how we could be of greatest use to the greatest number of men. And it followed that if three regiments in a brigade were in an attack, being with any one of the three would make it impossible to do anything in the other two. The converging point for the wounded would be the advance dressing-station of the Field Ambulance to which we were attached. But operations on the peninsula did not at all follow the book, and later on the principal chaplain laid it down quite clearly that, while under normal circumstances the above rule is the best to follow, each chaplain must use his own discretion and be where he feels he can be of greatest use. Since then the number of chaplains has been increased, which makes this easier. But there can be no ideal arrangement until each battalion has its own chaplain of the denomination of the majority, whose post shall be at the regimental dressing-station and who will share the life of the regiment as a non-combatant on the same standing as the medical officer and quartermaster.

The chaplain is a non-combatant, and surely it must be wrong for him to go out in the attack, much though he may hate not to share the danger of his men to the

29TH DIVISION CAMP AT MEX, NEAR ALEXANDRIA

(*Another view*)

full. His work comes after the attack, and perhaps most of all when the men come away tired and worn out for a little rest, or when they are spending those continuous days of wearisome strain in the trenches. And not least of all is the fact that he is the best channel of communication between the men and those at home. Very often one is asked to promise to write if anything happens, and the little personal letters the chaplain can write to those at home are most welcome, and the knowledge that all that can be done by decent burial has been done. These are only a few considerations brought out by after events.

D

CHAPTER IV

(April 9—24)

Friday, April 9.—We left Alexandria in the morning and went straight off without waiting as we had
expected. I held my two services as usual in the
evening. I knew nothing of the South Wales Borderers, and when I got into their dining-room had
some difficulty in collecting enough to sing a hymn,
but afterwards they gathered round in good numbers.
Next day there was a large crowd. I have been seeing
some of the men in my cabin. Some are very penitent.
We had lovely weather as usual. I have many argu-
ments with the officers, which are rather amusing.
Some of them spend most of the day mildly gambling
at poker. They argue that it is their form of recreation
of which they are passionately fond, and as their total
gains or losses are inappreciable it can do no harm.
However, I tell them quite plainly I think it would be
a good deal better if they neither gambled nor drank
even moderately, and they none of them agree, though
they acknowledge I am entitled to my opinion if asked
for it. They think me very broad-minded in my
teaching. They are such good, nice fellows, and so
easy to get on with. It is a great experience in learning how to deal with men. It seems so important to
know where to be broad-minded and where narrow.

Saturday, April 10.—We passed Rhodes and other islands.

Sunday, April 11.—I had a Celebration and three parades in the morning, and a voluntary service at night. I am getting to think more of parades. Men do listen, and, I think, pray. We arrived at Lemnos at midday. It is not nearly so hilly and barren as most of the islands. The slopes round the sea are beautifully green with growing crops. No trees though. There is a most wonderful, large, almost absolutely landlocked harbour. It was an extraordinary sight coming into it. A lovely fresh spring day, the great natural harbour with its fresh green shores, and the water simply covered with a mass of every kind of shipping. There was the *Queen Elizabeth,* looking quite new and untouched, a five-funnelled Russian battleship,[1] a large hospital ship (white, with red crosses), a number of strangely-shaped French men-of-war, and various other British ones, torpedo boats, submarines, water-plane boats, and a whole lot of transports of every conceivable kind, colliers, tugs, trawlers, lighters—in fact, every form of shipping. Eventually we took up our berth immediately along-side a transport. I went over it in the afternoon to see if I could hold a service. But there was no place. It was simply crammed, 350 horses and 600 men, and no quarters for them. They had to sleep on the decks, and the smell was not at all savoury. It was quite exciting watching a hydroplane circling round. In fact, something was going on all the time. We could see the shore dotted with funny little windmills used for crushing grain, and tents of Australian and French troops, and one or two villages.

[1] The *Askold,* soon christened by the men "The Packet of Woodbines," from her five long thin funnels.

Monday, April 12.—The General and Staff and Colonel went off on the *Queen Elizabeth* this morning to view the situation at the Gallipoli peninsula, and the men have been practising going down rope-ladders into boats and rowing, at which they were pretty bad. I determined to go ashore, and went off with two officers in a little native boat. We walked round the bay for two or three miles and got to Mudros, one of the chief villages. There was quite a decent road, with telephone wires, and many flocks of sheep and growing crops, and the place looked quite rich, but one missed trees. I wonder if we shall establish ourselves here. The trouble seems to be the anchorage, which is bad, as the soil is loose, and if there is a strong wind the ships drag their anchors. The village was a funny little place, with fairly solid stone houses and a really fine, large, imposing, new church. The natives had erected a number of little stands where they sold oranges, Turkish delight, figs and dates. We seem to have taken over the island, and natives have to get passports to enable them to go from one place to another. However, they must be making lots of money. Many can speak English, either having been on English merchant boats or to America. The two officers I was with were rather stupid, and discussed hunting, etc., most of the way, and seemed to take no interest in poking about. We had some difficulty in getting a boat to take us back, as they all wanted so much money. Eventually an English officer appeared and made a row and took their names down, and we sailed off in a fairly choppy sea, dropping a man at the Russian boat on the way.

Tuesday, April 13.—I went on shore again in the afternoon. It was very windy off shore, and the boat had the greatest difficulty in rowing the little way to

PRACTISING GETTING INTO BOATS FROM H.M.T. 'A——' IN
MUDROS HARBOUR

land. The General and Staff were in the boat, and it
was very funny seeing them carried ashore on the
backs of some of the Naval Division. It had been
raining all the morning, and the road, which had been
perfectly dry the day before, was a mass of slimy
mud, which made walking very difficult. I saw the
Commander-in-Chief tearing along through the village.
They say he always walks very fast, and is of a quick,
nervous disposition. We sailed back to the A——
in time for tea. I was pretty well occupied every
evening for the rest of the week. At 5.30, some four
or five men who had given me their names for Confirmation came in for a class; at 6.15 I went down to
hold a service for the Naval Division and Engineers.
Most of the former are pit-boys from Durham, nice
boys, and I enjoyed my meetings with them very
much. Two of the engineers came one evening and
asked to be baptized, so I had further to arrange
Baptism Classes. Then at 7, or as soon after as possible, I snatched some supper, and at 7.30 went to the
Royal Fusiliers, and at 8.15 to the South Wales
Borderers, and always had good gatherings. I went
very hot at them one evening on the moral question,
and told them quite plainly that victory in the war
would be of no use unless we learnt to change public
opinion with regard to it. In fact, I have been waging
incessant war against the whole thing, among the
officers just as much as amongst the men. They are
all very candid with me about it. However, it would
take too long to go into a discussion of the whole
question here.

Wednesday, April 14.—I did not go ashore any
more, as I was kept pretty busy on board one way and
another. I visited the *Implacable* (a battleship), however, going on board with a party of officers. I was

taken all over by the chaplain. He gave me some Prayer Books, for which I was glad. By the way, we moved our position on Tuesday, I think, and came alongside the B——, sister-ship to the A——, with two regiments, the Divisional Staff and Major-General Hunter-Weston, and no chaplain of any kind, so I was the only one among some 5000 men.

Thursday, April 15.—I kept quiet all day, and did not go off the boat. But somehow there always seemed a lot to do, with the various classes and services and endless people to talk to. We got two mails during the week, and it was very nice getting some news. Two books on Turkey and a sketching-case also arrived. I wonder if I shall get any opportunity of using it.

Friday, April 16.—I rowed over to the *C*——, which was tied up with the *D*——, and had the L.F.'s, Dublins, and Munsters on board between them ; and arranged to come over on Sunday afternoon and hold parades. I also saw the two R.C. chaplains, and discovered a C. of E. one, belonging to the Naval Division, who arranged to take the Celebrations. But I said I would like to see the L.F.'s again in the afternoon. I had got to know them so well. By now the harbour has become a perfect mass of shipping. There must be well over 100 transports, supply ships, hospital ships, some 20 men-of-war, besides colliers, mine-sweepers, water-boats, and tugs of all descriptions, and it is exceedingly difficult to find any boat one wants. All kinds of boat-drill has been going on. The men are not much good at rowing, and the boats are very heavy and cumbersome. But they are as a rule towed in strings of five or six by a steam pinnace.

It was, I think, this day that the first mishap occurred. I have only gathered the details in scraps

(yesterday from a survivor) since. Transports had
been arriving every day from Alexandria, unescorted.
Among them was the *M*——, with artillery and the
South Wales Borderers' transport on board. At
10 a.m. the men were all on deck with lifebelts on,
doing boat-drill. The officers were mostly below,
looking at maps. A torpedo-boat appeared on the
horizon flying the halt signal (but flying no flag, a
fact which must have been overlooked, as the ship
obeyed the signal). The men looked on with interest
till she came about 150 yards off and hoisted the
Turkish flag. The Captain called out that he gave
them ten minutes to take to their boats. She fired
three torpedoes, all of which missed! The crew and
men began to lower the boats, one of which fell from
the davits and caused many casualties. Presently
several of our torpedo-boats came up, and the Turk
absconded. She ran ashore on Chios and was blown
up there. The *M*—— picked up her boats and went
on her way—short in her complement of the poor
fellows drowned. It appears the torpedo-boat slipped
out of Smyrna harbour one night when it was being
guarded by some of our boats. Another is said to
have got out as well.[1]

Saturday, April 17.—I spent the morning arranging
Sunday services. I discovered H—— had been signalling over to the *B*—— about taking services
there, so decided I must see him. I had sent him a
letter some days before, and he had signalled an answer
back which I never got. So I rowed over to the
E——, where he was, and had a little confab with
him and a Methodist chaplain, L——. I found H——
had been over to see me, and we crossed, but I waited

[1] I leave this account for what it is worth, though it is only
second-hand and may be inaccurate in detail.

for him. He is senior chaplain to the Division. C—— had not yet arrived, so we had to arrange for his brigade, which were mostly on my two boats. In the evening I had a little discussion with the men, who were exceedingly responsive, but said it was quite impossible for a soldier to say his prayers or give up swearing, both of which they would do if they returned to civilian life. I think this exaggerated the real state of affairs.

Sunday, April 18.—A very busy and fairly tiring day. Celebrations for two ships at seven and eight o'clock (about sixty altogether), two morning parades on A——, two afternoon parades on C—— (L.F.'s and Munsters), two voluntary evening services on A—— and B——. At the latter two men were baptized. There must have been 300 present.

Monday, April 19.—Celebration at 6.30 (six present). I could not understand why the senior officers of the L.F.'s were over both Sunday evening and Monday morning. I discovered later their Colonel, who commanded the A—— coming out, is to go home owing to valvular disease of the heart. Poor man, he is absolutely broken. I saw him since, and he looked dreadful. He has always been very good to me, and has been an indefatigable worker. B——, a very good fellow, ably seconded by P——, is now in command. I slept part of the afternoon. After tea we had a concert on deck, given by the men of the *Implacable,* who got themselves up very elaborately and were quite good, though fairly lewd. Most of their officers were entertained to dinner by the R.F.'s. It was a little sad to see the middies, some only sixteen, drinking a good deal of whisky and smoking many cigarettes during the evening. I had a good deal of talk with the captain. They

BOAT PRACTICE IN MUDROS HARBOUR

gave the men a concert in the evening, and I had no
services.

Tuesday, April 20.—I got everything packed up,
as I was under orders to go to the *M*—— and join
my Field Ambulance. I quite forgot that on Monday
morning we had a conference of chaplains on board
the *E*——. The *S*——, with R—— and another
Presbyterian chaplain, a New Zealander who had been
transferred, C—— and D—— (R.C.), had pulled
alongside. So with H—— and L—— (Wesleyan) we
were seven altogether, and had a very pleasant little
gathering, prayers being said by H——, R—— and
D—— (C. of E., Presbyterian, and R.C.). We discussed all sorts of things, where we were to go and
what to do and how to work together, etc. We are not
to advance beyond the first dressing-station. As the
R.F.'s had to be the first to land, I had to leave them.
But it was blowing very hard, and the *M*—— was
some distance off in the outer harbour, and I could not
get a boat to take me, though I tried all day and tackled
every picket-boat that came alongside. However, it
gave me an opportunity to hold some final gatherings
on board in the evening. The officers all seemed very
sorry I was to leave them. We had had endless
discussions.

Wednesday, April 21.—Again I was packed and
ready to go off, and had my servant (whom the Colonel
of the R.F.'s very kindly allowed me to keep) ready
waiting. I practically had despaired of getting off,
when at last I found a picket-boat was going from
the *B*—— with some officers who had been over for
a conference. It was still blowing hard, and our
departure had been postponed for twenty-four hours
in consequence. I got off eventually about 5.30, with
all my kit. The troops had been rearranged, and half

a battalion of the Hants had come on board, and my cabin was wanted. So I got on board the *M*—— in the evening. There are only a few officers—about eighteen—here and various odd units, the transports of five regiments, part of the 89th Field Ambulance with the Colonel, and a company of Royal Scots, the only Territorial regiment in the Division. I knew three of the transport officers—nice fellows—before, and the R.A.M.C. doctors slightly. The boat is fairly comfortable, a Red Star Line boat. There are about 700 horses on board. A water-boat came alongside yesterday, and we took in twenty tons of water.

Thursday, April 22.—Presumably the expedition starts to-day, about four o'clock I understand, if the weather has moderated enough. I shall see the transports pass and we will follow later. It seems a perfectly desperate undertaking. I can hardly expect to see many of my men alive again. My present feeling is that the whole thing has been bungled. The Navy should never have started the bombardment without the Army. Now there has been no bombardment for some weeks. Meanwhile the Turks, under German direction, have perfected their defences. The aerial reconnaissance reports acres of barbed wire, labyrinths of trenches, concealed guns, maxims and howitzers everywhere. The ground is mined. In fact, everything conceivable has been done. Our men have to be towed in little open boats to land in the face of all this. Of course their landing will be covered by the Navy. But I simply dread the first few days. I felt so miserable saying good-bye. However, I don't suppose it can be much worse than what has been going on in France. Slaughter seems to be inevitable. We had a printed message from Hunter-Weston, our Divisional General yesterday.

He said the eyes of the world are on us, and we must be prepared to face heavy losses by bullets, shells, mines, and drowning. Cheery, isn't it? People's eyes seem perfectly open. My brigade is to land first. At least three-quarters, it seems to me, will probably be casualties the first day. They are quite prepared for it. I feel very gloomy about it all at the present moment. One thing I feel certain of, and that is that the men will do their duty and cover themselves with glory, even if they are to be exterminated; and even if they had gone to France it would have been the same. Extermination is going on everywhere, and nothing can stop it now.

I held a service in the saloon in the evening, and a number of men and officers came.

Friday, April 23.—I had a Celebration at 7.30. Only three present. Practically all Presbyterian or R.C. on board. The boats did not go out on Thursday as we expected. The wind had blown pretty hard all day, but I don't think that was the cause. Some of the officers rowed over to the transports and brought me back some letters. I sat on deck most of the day and read *Guy Mannering*, which I enjoyed. There is always a lot to watch. We are anchored at the mouth of the harbour close to the boom through which all the ships must pass. A number of French boats had anchored outside. Boats of all kinds kept passing all day. I had another service at six o'clock on the boat-deck. But it was rather interrupted, as the transports began to move out from the inner harbour, and when the *A*—— came I had to let the men go, and we all cheered. An aeroplane kept circling overhead, and battleships were passing. Only the *A*——, *C*——, and *D*—— with the 86th Brigade on board, seemed to go. We understand they are going to anchor off Tenedos and make some sort of demonstration next day, and the real attack and landing was to take place at dawn on Sunday. The nights are lovely. There is a half moon. All the boats are lit up. The searchlights play across the harbour mouth. The most wonderful sights are the hospital ships : one lay quite close to us, with red crosses and a large belt of green in electric light.

Saturday, April 24.—I have been on deck watching practically all day. There has been a great procession of boats. The most wonderful began at 2 p.m., when the men-of-war filed very slowly and silently out, one behind the other, quite close to us, headed by the *Queen Elizabeth.* She was quite magnificent, with her eight huge 15-inch guns, in sets of four, piled on the top of each other. They were all cleared for action. There were seven men-of-war, followed by six destroyers. They made a most beautiful curve as they passed us to go through the boom. The sun shone out and they gleamed. It was an unforgettable sight. Some of the ships had a number of Australians on board. We waved and cheered occasionally, but it was mostly quite silent. Then came many more transports towing lighters, mine-sweepers, and tugs of all kinds among them. What a tremendous business it all is ! A large number of boats have anchored just outside the boom. We are to move out at 6.20 a.m. to-morrow. The attack presumably will start at dawn. It will be a great joy if we find even half the 86th Brigade in the firing-line when we land. I feel a little more hopeful now. Everything possible seems to have been done, and the victory surely will be ours if it is for the good of the world that it should be. The transports of the 86th Brigade are on board,

BOAT PRACTICE, MUDROS HARBOUR, WITH TOW OF BOATS AS AT LANDING

and the officers and men feel very sick at being left behind and seeing their regiments pass. We hear there is to be a most terrific bombardment of about 120,000(?) shells. The troops are to land in every manner of way. We will come on the scene only when they have been able to advance at least five miles. The 87th and 88th Brigades will follow close on the 86th. No wounded can be carried off for forty-eight hours. I think that we all feel that we are the centre of the world, and that the war in France for the moment falls in the background. It is all the most extraordinary adventure. We have had messages from the King and Sir Ian Hamilton. None of us will ever forget that procession of men-of-war and transports. I talked a lot with the men this afternoon and with the officers on board. Well, I suppose we will know something soon.

CHAPTER V

(April 25—30)

SPECIAL BRIGADE ORDER
BY BRIGADIER-GENERAL S. W. HARE
COMMANDING 86TH INFANTRY BRIGADE

FUSILIERS,
   Our Brigade is to have the honour to be the first to land and to cover the disembarkation of the rest of the Division. Our task will be no easy one. Let us carry it through in a way worthy of the traditions of the distinguished regiments of which the Fusilier Brigade is composed; in such a way that the men of Albuhera and Minden, of Delhi and Lucknow may hail us as their equals in valour and military achievement, and that future historians may say of us as Napier said of the Fusilier Brigade at Albuhera, "Nothing could stop this astonishing Infantry."
            S. W. HARE, BRIGADIER-GENERAL,
                 Commanding 86th Infantry Brigade.

Sunday, April 25.—At 6.20 a.m. we weighed anchor on a beautiful calm morning and steamed slowly out of harbour. I had a Celebration at 7 a.m. and a service on deck at 9 a.m. As we finished we began to hear the first sounds of firing in the dim distance. Every one had their glasses out, and we fixed them on the horizon to the front of us. Gradually we made out the outlines of the Gallipoli peninsula and the mouth of the Dardanelles, and saw transports and battleships lying off all the way round and up the Dardanelles, and heard the sound of guns from the latter booming out louder and louder as we drew closer. We all knew pretty well the plan of campaign before we left Lemnos. Three landings were to be made on "V," "W" and "X" beaches on the point of the peninsula by the 29th Division. The French were to land on the Asiatic side and the Australians right up the Gulf of Saros (at least so we thought). You can imagine how we strained our eyes to see what had happened. We anchored right in the middle of the stream flowing out through the Dardanelles just three miles from the land. In front slightly to the left is the Gallipoli peninsula, with Cape Helles at the point, and a village, a lighthouse and forts. Across, on the right, is the Asiatic coast, with a large village on the top of a cliff on the sea, a sandy beach inside the Dardanelles and another village further up. The Gallipoli peninsula is precipitous all round except for one or two small beaches. Above the cliffs the land from the sea looks fairly level, sloping gradually up for a distance of five miles to a hill on the horizon, Achi Baba Dagh, about 600 feet high. As a matter of fact about a mile from the coast is a valley, really only a depression.

Well, both sides were receiving a tremendous bombardment from the men-of-war. They were demolishing forts and villages along the coast on either side, and through the glasses we could see them crumble away under the shells. The lighthouse on Cape Helles was demolished. We watched with special interest the Russian cruiser with five funnels demolish the village of Yeni Shehr on the Asiatic side. The *Queen Elizabeth* was about a mile up the Dardanelles, blazing away with her 15-inch guns, landing shells all

over and up onto the top of Achi Baba. Meanwhile
we could see that the landing had been effected by the
different troops on both sides. We could just make
out men on the beach. Just under the village and fort
of Sed-ul-Bahr we could see where a tramp steamer[1]
had been run ashore, as we had understood it would
be, the troops, I believe, jumping out of the sides,
which were to be let down. On " X " and " W " beaches
there were a lot of boats and lighters drawn up. We
could make out troops on the top of the cliff. The
men-of-war and many of the transports lay quite close
up to the shore, and there were a crowd of tugs and
picket-boats of all kinds about everywhere. We saw
no shell drop in the water and no boats seemed to have
been hit. We got no news for some time, however.
The first we heard was from the *F*——, which
anchored alongside and said she had landed her men
of the Naval Division without a casualty. We could
see rows of small boats put off to the hospital ships.
Later in the evening a destroyer passed and shouted
out that we had demolished five forts, and in some
places advanced three miles. This subsequently seemed
to be greatly over-estimated. It was a most extraordinary sight, laid out like a panorama in front of us,
and yet impossible for us really to know what was
happening. We could see French troops landing on
a sandy beach on the Asiatic side and artillery coming
into action. Our artillery had not landed yet. Our
eyes got tired out with straining to look through
glasses. I had another service at 8 p.m. in the saloon,
which was crowded mostly with Presbyterians, many
officers coming. The bombardment quieted down in
the evening and I went to bed about 10.30.

[1] The famous *River Clyde*, of course.

Monday, April 26.—I awoke at 1.45 a.m. to the sound of a terrific bombardment and almost incessant rifle fire. I put a coat on and went up on deck. I found a ship's officer on watch. I had been terrified of a counter attack by the Turks at night with our men exhausted. There was a terrific noise going on—almost incessant rifle fire and machine guns on both sides of the Dardanelles. I felt quite sickened, feeling how terrible the first night must have been for the men. I stayed there an hour, during which it went on all the time, watching the flashes of the guns. But it seemed no good going on watching, so I went to bed again at 2.45. Practically every one else had slept through it all. At breakfast of course we knew nothing except that there had been violent fighting, and could make nothing more out during the morning. It did not seem that we were making much advance. The bombardment continued intermittently. We could see the Turkish shrapnel burst over where our men must be. It was another beautiful day. I got tired of watching, however, and read a good deal. At last in the afternoon a tug came up with orders that we were to go within half a mile of "X" beach and land 160 boxes of ammunition, which was a very welcome change. As we got nearer we could see a well-established landing on "W" beach. Some wagons appeared to have been landed, and there was a fairly easy way up the cliffs. Crowds of men were moving about, landing stores. The R.A.M.C. had established a base and were tending wounded. We coasted along round the point to "X" beach, a much smaller one with no natural way up the cliff, where we saw the engineers busy cutting out a road. We had been told to look out for snipers, and some shots appeared to drop round the ship. We anchored off the coast (the Captain was very excited

E

and shouted a lot), and four boats put off with ammunition, getting ashore as ordered by four o'clock.   We
could see a large crowd on the beach, also landing
stores, and a R.A.M.C. station.

Well, at last we got some news from those who went
ashore, and also from a man of the Border Regiment,
who had just had his fingers shot off, while the boats
were there, by a sniper.   However, he was quite cheery
and I went and saw him in the evening.   Well, of
course this was only one beach and we could get no
general survey or really authentic news.   But what
came out most clearly was that my own two special
regiments had been terribly cut up, but otherwise the
casualties had not been heavy.[1]   In fact it was very
black about the R.F.'s and the L.F.'s.   The Borderers
had landed without mishap and supported the R.F.'s.
The wounded man said he had heard the R.F.'s roll
called that morning, and there were only about 240
that answered.[2]   The Colonel and two Majors were
said to be wounded and only nine officers left.   But it
is impossible to know any facts for certain.   On "W"
beach it appears that the L.F.'s were terribly cut up
on landing.   It was the obvious landing-place, and the
Turks had laid barbed wire in the water.   This we had
heard before.   Well, as soon as our boats got back we
weighed anchor and came back to our old position.   I
felt very blue.   My two particular regiments cut up
and I was not with them or even near them, and it
is impossible to hear any details.   It all sounds very
horrible.   I ought to have been there, at any rate on
the beach, seeing the poor wounded fellows and burying the dead.   There seems to have been no chaplain

---

[1] Of course this does not refer to the terrible landing at "V"
beach.
[2] There were really more than these.

"X" BEACH, WHERE 2ND ROYAL FUSILIERS LANDED, EARLY IN MAY, WHEN USED MAINLY FOR UNLOADING FLOUR FOR FIELD BAKERY

there.[1] But what can I do? I am ordered to be with
my Field Ambulance. Well, things were not so noisy
this night. It appears most of the firing the night
before had been wild and unnecessary, but I expect
every one's nerves must have been on edge and they
blazed away without reason. I am not surprised. The
landing must have been ghastly. However, on seeing
the cliffs the marvel is that they managed to land at
all. The enemy had known for months that they were
coming and had time to make every preparation. Two
regiments, and how many more we don't know, had to
be sacrificed to make the landing. There are five
transport officers on board, the four regiments of my
brigade having their transports here, and another. It
is bad for them being left in suspense while their regiments are being cut up.

Tuesday, April 27.—There seems to have been a
certain amount of bombardment during the night, but
when I woke up I saw the Russian and a French man-
of-war steaming away to the south, and all sound of
firing ceased on the Asiatic side. Later a French
torpedo-boat passed us, and when we asked how they
were getting on, they said, "C'est fini—déterminé,"
which sounds hopeful. No one paid us any attention
all day and we could get no news. I got tired of watching through glasses, and lay in a chair and read *Guy
Mannering* all day—an extraordinary occupation in
the middle of a terrific bombardment and while many
of one's recent friends lay mangled, dying, and dead.
But the only thing is to be philosophical. It is war,
and war must mean death, and it is no use getting agi-
tated. The fighting did not appear to progress very
rapidly. They did not get anywhere near the top of

[1] I discovered later that both H—— and L—— had landed on
the Sunday, and had been working heroically.

Achi Baba. We could see shrapnel burst everywhere
and at intervals the men-of-war started bombarding
certain points on the horizon or lower slopes of the hill.
Shrapnel seemed also to be bursting over where our
men presumably were. We had been delighted the
evening before to see nine French transports come up
crowded with men, and also an English one with part
of the R.N.D., evidently to reinforce us. Our artillery
were well in action all day and the nearer slopes seemed
quite safe. But as this is a transport ship they will
not want us till all is cleared of the enemy. Besides,
the beaches are small and crowded with more important
units landing. We saw masses of troops moving all
along the tops of the cliffs, in some cases running
back as though being shelled, possibly reserves exposing themselves a little too freely. But it was impossible to make anything out for certain and one gets
tired of guessing. We keep wondering what the Australians are doing. Again it was a lovely day and
the whole thing seemed like a sort of show. It blew
rather a squall in the evening, but calmed off com-
pletely at night, and was quite warm with a brilliant
full moon. The ships were all lit up and everything
was perfectly peaceful. I suppose some day we shall
know something. I wish I knew the fate of the R.F.'s
and L.F.'s for certain. Perhaps it may not be as bad
as we imagine; but I am afraid it must be very bad.
I should have been there, and wonder if I should not
have insisted on staying on board the *A——*. But
that is unprofitable speculation now.

Wednesday, April 28.—Another day of waiting with
absolutely no news. Again a beautifully fine day.
We have been wonderfully fortunate in our weather.
Again we watched through glasses all day. The battle
seemed to rage on both sides of Achi Baba. We

THE RUSSIAN CRUISER, THE 'ASKOLD,' SOON NICKNAMED BY THE
MEN "THE PACKET OF WOODBINES"

GENERAL VIEW OF PENINSULA LOOKING TOWARDS MORTO BAY

could see shrapnel bursting everywhere, but it was really impossible to be certain whether it was our own or the enemy's! Later in the afternoon the battleships started dropping shells on the further side of Achi Baba. At about 6.30 a most tremendous bombardment started from a number of battleships on three sides of the promontory. Up to the north we could see a captive balloon moored to a ship which was apparently directing operations. Not far from it, well out to sea, was the *Queen Elizabeth*. Two or three battleships up the Dardanelles were firing away with tremendous rapidity. They seemed to be sweeping along the whole top of the Achi Baba range, evidently covering a big infantry advance. The sun was setting and lit up the whole promontory, evidently giving a good light for observations. The bombardment lasted about an hour or less, and must have been terrific for those on the hill. After supper the wind got up and raged very strong all night and turned pretty cold, but as it was off shore and with the current it did not seem to make any waves, so we had a calm night. We are all longing to land and get some news. All the world must know much more than we do only a few miles away from the scene of action. What are the Australians doing? How is the Navy getting on further up the Dardanelles? We know nothing.

Thursday, April 29.—This is a perfectly interminable wait. Day after day passes and we get no news and no orders. It was very quiet on land till evening, when a slight bombardment of the right-hand shoulder of Achi Baba took place, but the battle seemed to have got a good deal further away and the shells to be dropping mostly on the further side. We saw practically no shrapnel burst. There was a little fighting on the Asiatic side. It turned calm again in the afternoon and was dead calm at night, with a perfectly gorgeous full moon rising behind the Asia Minor mountains and shining on the sea, while the sun set in an absolutely clear sky. I wrote a letter home as I felt I must go on doing so, hoping that some day a chance of posting them may come. I am personally quite happy to be anywhere, but it seems a ridiculous waste of time. Three or four transports came up in the evening, and seem to have put in to shore while we are still left here. It seems quite inexplicable why they send us no orders.

Friday, April 30.—Just after breakfast the Turks started to bombard the French base camp on " V " beach. We could see about half-a-dozen shells drop apparently right in the centre of their camp where they had a number of tents pitched, and quantities of horses picketed and hundreds of men about. One shell seemed to come from the Asiatic side. As far as it was possible to see through the telescope comparatively little damage was done, men were calmly walking about, the tents seemed undisturbed, and the tramp steamer, which had been run ashore, appeared to be none the worse. The Turks seemed to have planned a general bombardment, as shells appeared to come from the other side of Achi Baba, and shrapnel to burst all over the slopes on this side. Several shells dropped in the water in the Dardanelles close to the battleships. The ships all started to reply, and before long the batteries on the Asiatic side were silenced, or ceased to fire, and shells have been dropping intermittently on the slopes of Achi Baba. But everything is conjecture at this distance. It is a gorgeous morning and turning much warmer.

The following account has been contributed by Lieut.-Colonel Newenham commanding the 2nd Royal Fusiliers.

CLIFFS ABOVE "X" BEACH, WITH ROYAL FUSILIERS, ON APRIL 25, SHORTLY AFTER THE LANDING

Left to right. Lt.-Col. Newenham (wounded later that day), Capt. Shafto the Adjutant (killed a week later), and an Orderly.

On *April* 23, by night, the ships containing the
covering force—*i. e.* 86th Brigade (2nd Royal Fusiliers, 1st Lancashire Fusiliers, 1st Royal Munster
Fusiliers, and 1st Royal Dublin Fusiliers)—sailed to
Tenedos, where we lay on the 24th, and completed
necessary transfers of men and warships, etc.

Half Battalion Royal Fusiliers and Headquarters
went on board H.M.S.*Implacable* about 7 p.m., from
which ship we had been practising getting into boats,
and so on; the other Half Battalion, under Brandreth,
spent the night on two Fleet mine-sweepers. At about
10.30 p.m. the brigade and warships all sailed for
the peninsula, arriving there by night. We had a
good breakfast on *Implacable* at 3.30 a.m. We then
proceeded to load up the boats, four tows of six
boats each and a steam pinnace, twenty-five to thirty
men in each boat, besides the six bluejackets to row
when the pinnace cast us off.

April 25.—At 4.45 a.m. the bombardment by the
Fleet began, twelve or fourteen battleships, including
Queen Elizabeth with her 15-inch guns, all blazing
away, a tremendous din, but nothing to when we
landed. At about 5.15 a.m. we started off in our
tows, with our mother-ship, *Implacable,* in the middle,
like a most majestic eagle and her brood.

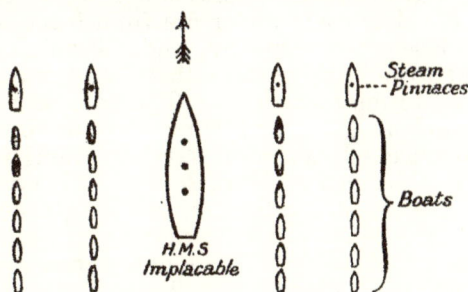

The Captain of the *Implacable,* Lockyer, was splendid—they were all top-hole; he had his anchor over

the bows with a bit of spar, and took his ship right in along with our boats till the anchor dragged; we all thought it splendid, and it most undoubtedly saved us many losses in the boats and landing.

All the officers and men of *Implacable* were most awfully good to us, they fed the men in the evening and gave them a splendid meal at 3.30 in the morning, which made all the difference to them in the bad time coming.

However, to continue: while we (W and X Companies) were being towed towards our beach called "X," the remaining Half Battalion, Y and Z Companies, on the mine-sweeper, were coming on; they were to come in as far as the vessel could go, and then be landed by the same boats which had put us ashore. As we got to shore the *Implacable* raised her sights and fired further over our heads.

We got off very lightly while getting ashore; I can only put it down largely to the way our mother-ship plastered the beach for us at close range; however, we had our bad time later on. About 100 yards from the shore the launches cast us off and we rowed in for all we were worth till the boats grounded, then jumped into the water, up to our chests in some places, waded ashore and swarmed up the cliff, very straight but, fortunately, soft enough for a good foothold. We then came under fire from front and both flanks. I sent one company, under Frank Leslie, to left front to hold them back there, and one straight ahead and to the right front. The fire was very hot, rifles, machine guns and shrapnel, and our losses heavy at once. I can never say half enough for the gallantry of the men under these trying circumstances. They lost most of the leaders, but fought on splendidly just the same. In the meantime, the other Half Battalion was landing behind us. I had orders to join up with the Lancashire Fusiliers, who were landed on "W" beach. I knew they had had a terrible time in the boats, as they were next to us going ashore. I collected all I could, after holding the left and front and leaving a reserve Company, to bring ammunition, water, etc., up the cliff, and moved to attack Tekke Hill; this we eventually captured on our side with the bayonet, losing heavily, at about noon. The *Implacable* was so close in that we heard her crew cheering us after the attack.

I got signal communication with the brigade about 7 a.m., and with the K.O.S.B. at "Y" beach later, to say they and the R.N.D. Battalion had landed but could not join up with us. I also learned that the landing on "V" beach was rather hung up. It was, therefore, most important to hang on to our bit. About 3 p.m. our centre, which was unavoidably rather weak, was being driven back. I got a message to "X" beach, where 87th Brigade were now landing, and eventually we were supported by some of the Border Regiment.

I had been wounded earlier, and now managed, with the help of Crowther, my servant, to get into cover and get "first aided." Incidentally we were very nearly cut off, but just saved the situation by the arrival of the Borderers.

We lost Frank Leslie, Scudamore, Brickland, de Trafford killed, and twelve other officers wounded, before early afternoon.

Our brigade was temporarily "washed out," the remains of my Battalion joining the Hampshire Regiment to form one Battalion.

On May 10 we had lost 20 officers and *about* 800 men.

I am able to publish the following accounts of the landing on "W" beach, later known as Lancashire landing, by three senior officers of the 1st Lancashire Fusiliers who were afterwards killed.

"As the boats touched the shore, a very heavy and brisk fire was poured into us, several officers and men being killed and wounded in the entanglements, through which we were trying to cut a way.   Several of my company were with me under the wire, one of my subalterns was killed next to me, and also the wire-cutter who was lying the other side of me.   I seized his cutter and cut a small lane myself through which a few of us broke and lined up under the only available cover procurable, a small sand ridge covered with bluffs of grass.   I then ordered fire to be opened on the crests, but owing to submersion in the water and dragging rifles through the sand, the breech mechanism was clogged, thereby rendering the rifles ineffective.   The only thing left to do was to fix bayonets and charge up the crests, which was done in a very gallant manner, though we suffered greatly in doing so.   However, this had the effect of driving the enemy from his trenches, which we immediately occupied.   After a pause to reorganize the men we advanced, but were met with heavy fire from further positions.   One company was pushed onto a flank, and thus we succeeded in forcing the enemy back. Towards evening we made slight progress forward, when we got up entrenching tools and dug in.   During the night a violent counter-attack was made by the enemy against us.   But we stood firm and drove them back again.   Our casualties were very heavy.   In my company alone I had 95 casualties out of 205 men.   One of my platoons captured 13 Turks in one trench.   The officers and men who were killed were buried together, close to the beach in an enclosure. We are now much reduced in strength, but the spirit of the old corps is just as strong as ever it was."

Major Adams, who wrote this account, was buried just above the beach on May 11.   The regiment at one time hoped to erect a permanent monument on the beach to their comrades who fell there.   He was much beloved by his regiment, and led his company very gallantly till his end.   He had been twenty-five years in the regiment.

TOP OF " X " BEACH, SHOWING ROYAL FUSILIERS SOON AFTER LANDING ON APRIL 25

From a letter from Captain H. R. Clayton who was killed on June 28 :—

"At 3 a.m. the morning of the 25th of April we had réveillé and breakfast about 3.30 a.m. At 5.30 we had to be all ready, and paraded and started to get into the ship's boats, each containing forty-five, including sailors to row. There were several pinnaces, and each towed four boats. As the sun rose straight in our eyes over the place we had to land, the pinnaces started for the shore with about 100 yards between, and each towing its four boats. During this time the ship's guns were pouring shells on the land. We thought nothing could live, but as a matter of fact they bombarded rather too far inland, and the trenches overlooking the landing beaches were not touched, though some yards of barbed wire on the beaches were torn up. About 200 yards from the beach the pinnaces slipped the boats and the sailors rowed for the shore. Can you imagine us packed in our boats quite defenceless, getting nearer and nearer and wondering when Hell would be let loose?

"They let us off a lot, thank God, as they did not fire until the boats began to ground, and the rifles and machine guns poured into us as we got out of the boats and made for the sandy shore. There was tremendously strong barbed wire where my boat landed. Men were being hit in the boats and as they splashed ashore. I got up to my waist in water, tripped over a rock and went under, got up and made for the shore and lay down by the barbed wire. There was a man there before me shouting for wire-cutters. I got mine out, but could not make the slightest impression. The front of the wire by now was a thick mass of men, the majority of whom never moved again. The trenches on the right raked us and those above us raked our right, while trenches and machine guns fired straight down the valley. The noise was ghastly and the sights horrible. I eventually crawled through the wire with great difficulty, as my pack kept catching on the wire, and got under a small mound which actually gave us protection. The weight of our packs tired us, so that we could only gasp for breath. After a little time we fixed bayonets and started up the cliffs right and left. On the right several were blown up by a mine. When we started up the cliff the enemy went, but when we got to the top they were ready and poured shot on us. After a breather in the enemy trenches above, we pushed on along the open and had an awful time. The place was strewn. I could see them being shot all round as we lay before advancing again. To make matters worse when I got ashore on landing I got out my glasses to look about, but they were full of water and I could see nothing; my watch stopped and has not gone since; the men's rifles were so clogged with sand that they could not use them."

The following letter is from Major Shaw, of the 1st Lancashire Fusiliers, to his brother. Major Shaw was killed on June 4.

"What can one say, and where can one begin, after ten days and nights of hundreds of hairbreadth escapes from death? To-day is the first time since landing that I have been out of the firing line night or day, and when I say the firing line I mean the enemy never more than 1000 yards from one. Put your head up out of the trench, whizz goes a bullet from an invisible sniper with telescopic sights; walk about outside, and bang goes a shrapnel close to you. The word is, ' Get in and get under; dig like mad.' I write this in a dug-out in the Divisional Reserve, with an unpleasant dust-storm blinding me. To-day is a holiday, and I have been to the sea and had a swim; my last wash was on board a battleship. Plenty of rations, not much water, no marching, but nervous exhaustion, and no sleep, that is the trouble as of yore. I always have and still contend that you cannot get used to being under fire; it is purely a case of hardening your-

"W" BEACH SOME DAYS AFTER LANDING OF LANCASHIRE FUSILIERS, LATER KNOWN AS LANCASHIRE LANDING

Note exposed position of horses, later heavily shelled; also battleships and transports moored before arrival of submarines.

self for the worst and shoving along. This is not
trench warfare. We have been in the open till a few
days ago, and are just on the defensive *pro tem*. If
we move we expect to gain at least two miles of
country. The enemy have been hurling themselves
against our trenches nightly. Rockets going, guns
banging, and a roar of rapid fire commencing at dusk
and ceasing at dawn. The last time (night before last)
they had a real go at us. We did well : heaped up
200 dead and captured 100. Our small band of
remnants cannot be budged. We hardly lost a soul
in this effort. I was very pleased. The second day
in attack I was sniped in the fleshy part of the right
knee—clean hole, but not lamed much, so have not
been out of action or reported wounded, and am now
healed up. The enemy got through the British line
once, and the French once by night, but were ejected
by the reserves, so no harm done. Shouts of ' Allah !
Allah ! ' and terrific uproar ; most exciting this was.
I only wished at the time you could have been with
me to see it. I suppose by the time you get this our
historical landing will have been written up in the
papers. The Naval johnnies say we accomplished the
impossible, and the name of that bay is to be the
' Lancashire Landing,' in our honour. I hate even
thinking about that scene of carnage, but, to oblige
you, I will unburden myself for the last time while I
have the chance. The *Euryalus* did everything they
could to make us comfortable that night, and after a
good breakfast we took to the boats at 4 a.m. The
fleet closed in at daybreak, not a breath of wind, a
beautiful warm summer morning, most peaceful scene,
and as it grew lighter we clearly discerned the land
about two miles off. We knew well we were in for a
dangerous venture ; everybody was in a state of ten-
sion, but quite cheerful, especially the boat's crew. I
had six sailors (three killed, I hear), and thirty-five
men of my Company, Headquarters Q.M.S., Sergeant-Major, Rangetakers, Signallers, Observers, and
2nd Captain Maunsell. They (the Headquarters) are

all casualties—I believe killed. My boat was in the
centre of the line. The ships started a tremendous
bombardment, and kept it up as the steam pinnaces
towed us ashore. The enemy made no reply; the
place might have been deserted. About 200 yards
from the beach the tows were cast off and the boats
shot ahead in line, and the sailors rowed like mad.
At about 100 yards from the beach the enemy opened
fire, and bullets came thick all round, splashing up
the water. I didn't see any one actually hit in the
boats, though several were; e. g. my Quartermaster-
Sergeant and Sergeant-Major sitting next to me; but
we were so jammed together that you couldn't have
moved, so that they must have been sitting there dead.
As soon as I felt the boat touch, I dashed over the side
into three feet of water and rushed for the barbed wire
entanglement on the beach; it must have been only
three feet high or so, and three bays, because I got
over it amidst a perfect storm of lead and made for
cover, sand dunes on the other side, and got good
cover. I then found Maunsell and only two men had
followed me. On the right of me on the cliff was a
line of Turks in a trench taking pot shots at us, ditto
on the left. I looked back. There was one soldier
between me and the wire, and a whole line in a row on
the edge of the sands. The sea behind them was
absolutely crimson, and you could hear the groans
through the rattle of musketry. A few were firing.
I signalled to them to advance. I shouted to the
soldier behind to signal, but he shouted back, ' I am
shot through the chest.' I then perceived they were
all hit. I took a rifle from one of the men with me
and started in at the men on the cliff on my right,
but could only fire slowly, as I had to get the bolt
open with my foot—it was clogged with sand. About
this time Maunsell was shot dead next to me. Our
men now began to scale the cliffs from the boats on the
outer flanks, and I need only add it was a capital
sight. They carried the trenches at the top at the
point of the bayonet : there was some desperate work

up there. In the trench I had been firing at, the enemy touched off a land mine just too soon, but the people near it, I hear, are deprived of speech, and deaf. This released me, and I collected about thirty men and pushed on up the hollow to my objective, point 318, where I got about 5 p.m. After some further hair-raising experiences, we entrenched there for the night. I shall not re-read this. I hate to think about it. Perhaps some time, if I am spared to join you, we may go over it again together, so please do not destroy it or have it published.

"I fear we are in for a wet night when this dust ceases. It is hot by day, and very cold about 5 a.m. I generally get up and beat my arms *à la* cabman about this time. It is a shame to fight here. It is highly cultivated : vines, corn, and patches of heather, and all sorts of wild flowers. The trees are very small, only twelve to fifteen feet high. All the farm-houses are blown to blazes. Be happy and comfortable at home. You miss the excitement, but you are spared much. Hoping you are all well, as I am so far, and with love to every one."

Sir Ian Hamilton, writing to a friend, commenting on this letter, says—

"I have mentioned Captain Shaw's name in my second dispatch, so his gallantry will not go unrecorded. As to his account written on May 5, it is the most live comment on the subject of the landing I have seen. Now that the gallant fellow is no more, I certainly strongly think you ought to have it published, for surely the embargo was only meant to prevent the bloom being taken off the story before the two brothers read it together."

His brother entirely agrees with this last sentence.

CHAPTER VI

ON CAPE HELLES

(*May* 1—5)

Saturday, May 1.—I have left my diary unwritten for a fortnight, and don't know how I shall ever catch up or give any connected or clear account of what has happened. I could write volumes if there were time.

We anchored close off "W" beach, now known as Lancashire landing, owing to the fact that the L.F.'s led the way and secured the landing there on Sunday, April 25, leaving over a hundred men dead on the beach. It is inconceivable, seeing the coast, how they ever managed to land. The whole story will be written some day, and as I can only give it second-hand it is hardly worth while to repeat it here. But we could not manage to get ashore that day. I decided to stay with the Field Ambulance, and land when they did. One boat-load managed to get ashore, but there was no room for me, and they returned later with news and some naval officers and engineers also came aboard, and at last we heard what had actually happened, the absolutely desperate affair the landing had been, and the appalling cost of it all. I was relieved to hear that the R.F.'s had not lost as heavily as we had first heard, and that some 450 men and ten officers were still left, and that the L.F.'s, though they had fewer men, had all their senior officers left. The Dublins were the worst, with only one officer and 300 odd men left. Occasional shells were still dropping about the beach. The camp was becoming a very busy sight, roads being made and stores of all kinds, guns, horses, wagons, etc., being landed.

Sunday, May 2.—We anchored very much closer in and started unloading. I had services on board in the morning, and eventually decided I could wait no longer, and went ashore with all the kit I could carry in the afternoon. Some of the Field Ambulance had landed, and I left my things with them and found H——, with the 88th Field Ambulance next door. He said he had been having a most terrible time. He had just come back from the trenches, where he had been caught all night in the middle of a big battle. The Turks had been attacking all the time, and shells had been bursting all round them. They had been repulsed with considerable loss. He had gone out to hold a Celebration, but of course any service had been impossible. He had landed the first day and been through everything, and had, like every one else, a harrowing time. L——, the Wesleyan chaplain, was also there. They had mostly been helping the Field Ambulance and dressing the wounded. We walked up to the hill behind the camp and watched the battle. Practically no progress had been made since the Wednesday. Achi Baba had been very strongly fortified, and is a network of trenches and barbed wire, with machine guns and artillery everywhere. We then walked over to "V" beach, now only used by the French, where the Dublins and Munsters had landed and lost so terribly. There is a ruined castle and village there, and the tramp steamer, the *River Clyde*, which has been run aground, and from which the landing had been made with such disastrous results to the Dublins. Even poor Finn, the R.C. chaplain, had been killed, being

F

ordered to land in the first boat.(^{1}) There we met K——
the R.C. chaplain of the Munsters, who had been up in
the firing line with his regiment the whole time since
landing, and had just come away for a short change.
We returned to camp later to find a message had come
in to ask a chaplain to go out and bury some artillery
officers.   So R——, H——, and myself set out at dusk
along the Krithia road, and went about one and a half
miles to some pillars, and made inquiries for the burial-
party everywhere, but could get no directions.   Then
a battle commenced.   We were close to the French
lines, among a lot of trees, and the French 75's started
blazing away close to us, and the whole place was in
a perfect din as the Turks replied and the ships joined
in.   It became quite dark, and as we could find out
nothing we decided it was more expedient to retire.
We had to walk right into the mouth of the French
guns, which was fairly alarming.   Everywhere carts
and wagons, with Indians, French, and English, were
going up to the firing line with supplies and ammunition.   We passed a battalion of the Naval Division
waiting to go up to the firing line.   They looked such
boys, and seemed very bewildered.   I felt so sorry for
them.   I expected to feel much more alarmed than I
did.   I could only feel what an utterly senseless and
wasteful thing war was.   But it was all pretty miserable.

The battle raged harder and harder.   When we got
back the other two went to bed, but I wandered about
the camp a little and got my dug-out ready.   I had got
all my kit ashore.   It turned pretty cold at night.   The
88th Field Ambulance was immediately next to ours.
They had not got ours into working order yet.   But
about 11 p.m. in poured the wounded to the 88th, and
about 25 came at once.   Their tents were already full

and they had used up all their blankets, and for some
time these poor wretches had to be left lying in the
open. I went round a little, but there was a good deal
of confusion, and as it was not my Field Ambulance
I felt I should only be interfering and could do no
good, and went off to bed feeling pretty miserable.

(¹) I leave this as I wrote it at the time. I have since
heard that Father Finn asked to be allowed to land
with his men, and had been put into one of the first
boats, and was shot either getting off the boat or immediately after getting ashore. The men never forgot
him and were never tired of speaking of him. I think
they felt his death almost more than anything that
happened in that terrible landing off the *River Clyde*.
I am told they kept his helmet for a very long time
after and carried it with them wherever they went.
It seemed to me that Father Finn was an instance of
the extraordinary hold a chaplain, and perhaps especially an R.C., can have on the affections of his men
if he absolutely becomes one of them and shares their
danger.

At a chaplains' meeting held some weeks later, two,
a Presbyterian and an R.C., undertook to see that
Father Finn's grave was properly tended. He was
buried close to the sea on "V" beach, and a road had
been made over the place. I think they managed to
get the grave marked off with a little fence.

Monday, May 3.—I awoke to find the wounded had
mostly been stowed away under some sort of shelters,
but there were crowds of them lying about. The rest
of my Field Ambulance had not landed yet. So after
hanging about a bit I went over to "X" beach where
the R.F.'s had landed, and found E—— the quartermaster. He greeted me with the sad news of Shafto's
(the adjutant) and Anstice's (²) deaths. Would I go up

and bury them? Of course. The regiments had just come into reserve, and he said he was going up himself, so off we went about one and a half miles inland, and found what was left of them—six officers and 435 men—in a vineyard. They had just come out of the firing line for the first time since landing. But they were wonderfully cheerful. It was quite a joy to be with them again. They had just lost four officers, Shafto and Anstice killed, M—— and B—— wounded, and this left J—— in command, and Mundy as adjutant, Hugget as machine-gun officer, and with Z——, T——, and G—— they made a very happy little family.([3]) J—— has made a simply capital C.O., and was full of praise of Mundy. Of course all were overwhelmed by Shafto's death. He was a universal favourite and a particularly charming man. He had already been buried, and his grave was near the firing line, so I could not very well get there.([4]) They were very delighted to see me. I next saw the brigade staff. Colonel —— of the South Wales Borderers was acting as Brigadier, as the general had been wounded the first day, and F——, whom I was delighted to find alive, was Brigade-Major in place of Frankland([5]) who had been shot landing.

I made my way up towards the firing line to a gully —or nullah, as they are called here—only about 500 yards behind it, where N—— of the R.F.'s, and Q—— of the L.F.'s had their regimental dressing-stations. There was an absolute lull in the battle all day. The Turks were out everywhere, burying their dead, with white flags, and our men were walking about cooking their meals in the firing line, and it was a wonderfully peaceful scene. I found N—— absolutely tired out. He had had a very trying time ever since landing, and been under fire practically all the time. I said, as his

ROYAL FUSILIERS' MACHINE GUNS IN CENTRE OF CAPE HELLES IN MAY

regiment was in reserve, he had much better come
down to the beach with me and see the Field Ambulance, which, as it had not landed, had been unable
to help him. It seemed ridiculous his staying up
there. So he walked down to the beach with me and
his servant and two sick men. He had been thoroughly
shaken, and no wonder, poor fellow—no sleep, constant fighting, and all alone with the stretcher-bearers
and servant, all of whom I think had imposed upon
him. We found that the Field Ambulance had at
last all landed. The shock of landing had been so
great they had not been able to adjust themselves.
Practically all on the Brigade Staff had gone, and no
one seemed to know what to do. It was all rather
terrible.

Well, I got my things and returned to the regiment
with N—— for the night. We moved his aid post to
a place some way behind the reserve trenches, as it
turned out worse than where he had been before, and
he had the worst night of all, poor fellow. I lay in
a dug-out with three other officers. But I did not
sleep a wink. I could not have imagined such a
shindy. It started about 9.15 and went on till 6.15
next morning, and the longest pause I counted was six
seconds when there was no firing. In the trenches
the firing of rifles and machine guns was ceaseless
the whole night. The ships' guns and our field
artillery were firing intermittently all night. One
gun close to us made a terrible row. About one mile
away the French 75's were going all the time, sometimes firing, as we timed it, as many as fifty rounds
a minute. Then, of course, the Turks were replying
all the time with shrapnel. One, at least, I saw burst
just above us, but most burst behind or to our left,
where I discovered one or two men had been wounded

in the trenches. The others slept peacefully through it all, they were so worn out. It was a strange experience. I did not feel particularly alarmed, but the night seemed pretty interminable and the noise only to get more terrific towards morning. I got up and watched the shrapnel bursting everywhere. But we have all discovered by now that the Turkish shrapnel does very little damage except during an actual advance at close range. I doubt if ours does much more. Provided you are well dug in you seem pretty secure against everything. It is only during an advance that men get badly cut up. The snipers have been terribly bad. They are painted green and hide in holes in the ground surrounded by branches, and have masses of ammunition, food, and water with them, and just wait their opportunity to pick off people. But I am attempting only to give a first-hand account, and if I were to tell everything I hear I would never stop. As far as I could make out all that night's cannonade had effected nothing, except a few wounded on our side. Of course we could not know how much damage it had done to the Turks. But I think it had been mainly the result of alarm.

(²) It is always interesting hearing the men's opinions of their officers. I do not think I heard any one spoken more highly of by the men of the Royal Fusiliers than young Anstice. Over and over again during the subsequent weeks they would say to me: "You should have seen Mr. Anstice! I reckon he deserves the V.C. if any one does. There was nothing he would not do for his men. Why, I saw him myself working like a nigger, and much harder than any of the men, carrying ammunition, water and rations, going about all up and down the line without a sign of fear. And we none of us thought he had it in him. But they never stop

talking about him now. We are all changing our
opinions about many people out here."

(³) I think nothing throughout my time on the peninsula struck me as so remarkable as the way in which
this handful of officers, with a junior captain as C.O.,
and little more than a boy as adjutant, handled their
regiment after the harrowing experiences they had
been through. They entered into it with such zest
and worked tremendously hard, overlooking nothing.
Mundy, who acted as adjutant, seemed to think of
everything. The smallest detail did not escape him.
His map-drawing was remarkable, and the quick way
in which he grasped a situation and saw what was the
best thing to do showed that he had real military
genius. And perhaps the most remarkable part was
that previously none of his brother officers realized he
had it in him. War seems to bring out so many latent
qualities. And the way in which J—— handled the
regiment, the wisdom and tactfulness he showed, his
power of winning immediately the confidence of officers
and men alike, the sane, calm judgment he displayed
throughout, are beyond all praise. I can only say
that under them the regiment, though so terribly de-
pleted in numbers, made not only an exceedingly happy
and enthusiastic family, but a really valuable fighting
unit.

(⁴) It was a deep regret to me that I was unable to
bury him. However, I had decided to go at the first
opportunity with some of the other officers and hold a
service at the grave. But he was buried in a very
exposed spot and this was impossible. It was not till
July 10, practically my last day on the peninsula, that
this was possible, as is recorded later.

I do not think I met any officer who won every one's
affections so quickly as Captain Shafto, the adjutant of
the Royal Fusiliers. Officers of many regiments in
the Division would ask : Who is that delightful adjutant with a smile always on his face, who is always
ready to do anything for any one? Many is the
time I worried him myself, but I never saw him

provoked or put out. He was always at every one's disposal.

(⁵) Major Frankland was quite one of the finest officers who came out with the Division. He had been out in France since the beginning of the war, and when he returned to take over duty as Brigade-Major of the 86th Brigade he was very much overstrained and suffering from sleeplessness. However, he threw himself into his work with indefatigable zeal, and was always at the service of any one who came to him. The voyage out considerably rested him, and it was with a fiery enthusiasm that he went off to the landing. The Brigade Staff landed on "W" beach. When Frankland saw the terrible time the L.F.'s were having he went straight up to the hill on the right, feeling the matter was becoming almost desperate, and utterly fearlessly walked along the edge of the cliff where he was killed. I afterwards saw his grave just at the top of the steep cliff by the lighthouse.

Tuesday, May 4.—In the morning it gradually calmed down. I had breakfast with the R.F.'s, and left them soon after preparing to return to the firing line. They were only allowed one night's rest. I felt very sad to say good-bye to them, but it was impossible to go into the firing line with them. I walked off along the line of the Munsters and Dublins. There are only a few Anglicans among them, and as Father K—— was there I did not stop much to talk to the men, but I was loaded up with a number of letters to post and commissions of various kinds. So few of them were left that they had been joined together to form one regiment, "the Dubsters." Only O'Hara, a young lieutenant of about twenty-three, was left of the Dublin officers. Ten had been killed, the rest wounded. He looked very harassed, poor boy! But I did admire him for having stuck it

OFFICERS OF ROYAL FUSILIERS, EARLY IN MAY, IN CENTRE OF CAPE HELLES.
SHRAPNEL WAS BURSTING TO THE RIGHT

Left to right. Author, J——, G——, Lieut. Mundy, T——, S——.

out as he had. He said he did not know how he had
got through it. I was very touched by him, and
promised to do anything I could to help.([6])

Then I returned to the beach and determined to try and
find the Colonel of the R.F.'s, who was wounded and
supposed to be on one of the ships. I got a boat and
rowed out to the C——. An elderly man also got in,
who turned out to be Josiah Wedgwood, who is out
here with a mounted machine-gun battery, and had
dismounted some of his guns and been in the firing line
close to the French. I saw a number of wounded
officers, including the Colonel of the Inniskillings, who
was very bad indeed, on the C——, and several who
were only slightly wounded and hoped to be back
soon, but I could not find the Colonel of the R.F.'s.
Evidently most of the wounded had been taken off to
Alexandria and Malta. Then I got on a mine-sweeper
and had some supper. The whole place was a mass
of unwashed wounded, hobbling about uncared for, as
there were only four doctors on board and they absolutely overworked. The mine-sweeper was full of
wounded they were bringing on board. There seemed
a tremendous number of them. A very large proportion have been slight cases fortunately, but I did long
to be able to give the men a good wash and a change
of clothes. Then I went on board the A——, where
I found M—— and T—— both expecting to be back
soon, and various others officers. They keep the mild
cases there. I hailed a steam pinnace which was
towing a number of wounded Turks and it took me
ashore.

([6]) I think it was quite wonderful how O'Hara
managed to get through those first few days. He most
thoroughly deserved the D.S.O., which, to the delight
of all who knew him, was given him later. Little

more than a boy, he had landed with his magnificent
regiment, the Dublins, in the most terrible of all the
landings on "V" beach, beneath the ruins of Sed-ul-
Bahr, which was full of machine guns which swept the
beach, and the most appalling wire entanglements were
spread all over. The next day they had to take the
castle with the bayonet, after which he found himself
the only officer left. He had then to lead what was left
of his regiment up into the centre of the firing line,
and remain there till May 3. He told me what he felt
most was the loneliness of it all. All his brother
officers were gone. He had no one to talk to. The
sergeant-major, who had been simply splendid and
his right hand, was killed by a sniper the next day.
O'Hara told me he felt his whole outlook on life had
been changed, and he could never be the same again.
I was deeply grieved to hear he died of wounds at
Suvla.

Extract from a letter of the Brigade-Major, 86th
Brigade, dated May 22, 1915, regarding the 2nd Royal
Fusiliers :—
"Where all have done well the Royal Fusiliers have
been beyond praise. With six junior officers and
about 400 men they have never lost their form for a
minute. Not only have they always done what might
have been expected of them, but they have risen to a
standard of soldiering which could not be higher, and
never departed from it. I am filled with admiration for
them. . . . The Royal Fusiliers, as I said earlier, have
done magnificently. They have lost none as prisoners.
In the night of 1/2 May, when the Turks broke our
line, they saved the situation with the bayonet."

Wednesday, May 5.—After hanging round camp
during the morning (I think I was at the Casualty
Clearing Station [C.C.S.]; probably I also went over to
"X" beach and saw Harding) I went up to the L.F.'s,
who had come out into reserve the night before. I

found all the senior officers still there. They had had six officers killed; but only a little over 300 men left. They were very glad to see me and gave me various commissions. I wandered down to the 88th Brigade Headquarters. The brigades were all being changed. I found a very depressed staff-captain, who said, "Where are the padres? Why don't they come and see us?" When I returned to the L.F.'s it was to find they were to go off to the firing line that very evening, much to their disgust. I said good-night to them as they gradually dribbled off to escape observation. I felt very gloomy seeing them go off, and returned sad and depressed to camp.

From a letter dated May 5 :—

"I am sending a large batch of diary which I hope will reach you some day. Of course it does not give news since I landed, which I managed to do at last on Sunday evening. I feel I could write books on my doings since then. I am most interested to find how all my horror and a great deal of my cowardice has left me. I have not seen any particularly grue-some sights yet, nor been in any real danger, so I have not had a severe testing. I think one of the stupidest things about the inconceivably appalling stupidity of war is the way life is squandered to no military pur-pose, simply by reasonable precautions being neg-lected. I suppose you will have seen the casualty lists. Well, I forbear all comments. I am quite callous. In fact the strange thing, I find, is that I am really extremely happy, though, as I say, I have not had anything bad to shake me. There is more good-ness and true unselfishness and seriousness about on this blood-stained peninsula than there is at a race-meeting, for instance, and that seems the only thing after all that matters. It is no excuse for war, but it makes it quite possible to be happy in it. The men, especially my two regiments, are really simply won-

derful after what they have been through. Men who
were at Mons say that was nothing to it. One of the
Irish regiments in my brigade has only one officer
left. I don't think anything more ghastly can be conceived than the landing. The great thing, in my
opinion, is that the weather has been so fine (though
the nights are cold), and every one is well. I feel
so sorry for the Turks, because I am sure they hate it
all so. I wish I could talk to their wounded. Of
course the strain on my regiments who have been in
the firing line without one night out since they landed
is terrible, especially now they are less than half
strength. But I wish you could have seen the junior
captain of one regiment who was left in command and
five other officers (out of twenty-four) handle their regiment, as I saw them do. They might have been born
to it. But officers should not be married; though I
think if they are not they think of their mothers just
as much.

"I am coming back to the base at nights now, as I
find there are so many commissions for me to under-
take for officers and men that it is the best plan, and
also I can do better if I sleep, which was utterly impossible in that shindy on Monday night. I think, if
I might perhaps make a suggestion to everybody who
cannot take a direct part in war, it is that there is really
no need to feel miserable about it. Of course everybody hates and loathes it here and only longs for it
to finish, but I think the real reason is that they feel
it is such an utter misuse of their lives, not so much
from fear: and on the whole nerves are wonderfully
absent. I think what I really mean to say is, that sin
and evil alone should make us feel miserable, and I
have never felt their absence as much as since I landed
here. If people lose those they love, may they not
have at least the supreme consolation that the vast
majority of them have died better men than they were
before? And after all goodness is the only thing that
matters, is it not? All the old scriptural phrases seem
to have a new meaning. Men are born again. Their

sins are forgiven—for they love much. All are kind
and considerate and really think least of themselves,
or if they don't the fact is very conspicuous and
rare. Don't think I don't mind these dear fellows
being killed. When I said good-bye to one regiment
which had at last had one day out of the firing line
and was unexpectedly ordered back there while I was
with them, though still tired out and longing for a
good rest, it was very hard—I cannot tell you how hard,
but it was not depressing. As I walk about and the
guns blaze away all round, and the ships pour their
large shells onto a little hill, and every possible con-
trivance that it seems possible to imagine is being put
into use, and I realize the labour, and time, and cost,
and brains involved, I only think of the waste and utter
madness and stupidity of it all. But after all it is no
worse than the energy expended in growing rich.
Well, I seem to be wandering, but the meaning of
life and death and things in general is so much more
interesting than what is actually happening—though I
own that has a very strong, but really I think only
passing, interest. I feel my experience and sympathies
so tremendously widened during the last three days. I
am afraid I shall have very horrible sights to see soon,
as we have got to get through at any cost, and we all
know what that means."

CHAPTER VII

A THREE DAYS' BATTLE, AND AFTER

(May 6—14)

Thursday, May 6.—My regiments had all gone up to the firing line. There was to be a big general attack all along the line, beginning at 11 a.m. The French were to start on the right. I had found my groom the day before, and decided to ride off and see what was about to happen. I rode down the West Krithia road to where some artillery horses were, and decided it would be best to tie up and then go off in search of the Field Ambulance dressing-station, which I understood was close by. I tramped a long way, but could get no trace of it. Meanwhile, the artillery was blazing away for all it was worth. Eventually I made my way back to camp, where I lunched, and then went off and got my horse and rode over to the dressing-station, which I now heard was on the main Krithia road, just this side of the towers among the trees. I got to them about three o'clock, and stayed till about six. The wounded were coming in pretty thick. There were three ambulances side by side, the 88th and 89th and the Naval Division, all among the trees in a little gully through which the road goes. There were lovely fig and pear trees round us, and little terraced gardens. The majority of the wounded were Naval Division, especially the Howe and Hood Battalions. They must have lost heavily. The Colonel of the Howe (I think) was killed. The wounded who came in at first were the slight cases mostly, who walked in from their regimental dressing-stations. There were also some of the L.F.'s and other regiments, but the R.F.'s were mainly being taken another way. It was very difficult to know what to do. Either the wounded were able soon to hobble off to the C.C.S., or they were so bad that they were given morphia. The latter cases were very few. One poor fellow had been shot through the spine and was in agony. There were one or two officers. I wandered from station to station. There was a chaplain (I think Wesleyan) at the R.N.D. station. One of Asquith's sons was wounded that evening, but I did not see him. They seem to have made rather too rash and rapid an advance and got under shrapnel fire. But it is impossible to get news on such occasions. Some said, "We have got the Turks on the run"; others, "I cannot see we have gained much." The great question was, Were we in Krithia yet? The answers were confused. I am afraid we advanced nowhere more than 1000 yards, at a pretty heavy cost. I believe the French did fairly well on their wing.

Well, it did not seem that I was able to be of much help there, so I rode back to the camp to see the wounded as they came in. I went over to the C.C.S., and chatted as far as possible to the ones I saw. They were very crowded in tents, so that there was no floor space left, and it was difficult to talk to them. Either they were slightly wounded and cheerful, or badly and under the effects of morphia. There was a certain amount of confusion. However, it was impossible to do anything to make things better. The walking cases are cleared off to the ships as quick as possible, but the stretcher cases have to wait twenty-four hours.

So eventually I went off to bed, as most of the wounded had come in. I had by now got a tent to myself, until then having slept in the dining-tent. The battle went on raging, but one gets used to the sound of firing. Somewhere about one in the morning the Colonel woke me up and said he would need my tent, as more wounded were coming in; the C.C.S. was full, and they would have to open up. So I got all my things out as quickly as possible, and then went to see if I could help. I think it was about twenty or thirty wounded we had in that night. They came in pretty cold and miserable, but the orderlies soon had beef-tea and bovril ready, and covered them with blankets, and made them as comfortable as possible, and they were soon soundly off to sleep. So I turned in again (into my sleeping-bag, that is to say), and followed their example.

Friday, May 7.—As there had been so much fighting, I imagined there must be various funerals, and was very anxious to know what had happened to my regiments. So I rode off with my groom to see if I could get up at least to the regimental dressing-stations. I went along the West Krithia road, past the Pink Farm, and then into a deep gully leading towards the firing line. When I had got the horses down into it, I left them with the groom and started to walk up the gully. On the way I met K——, who had just left the Munsters. They had not been in the thick of the fighting, but a good deal of shooting was still going on. Stray bullets were whistling about, and some went uncomfortably close. However, I wanted to get up if possible, until one or two came so close I decided it would be wiser to return. I found K—— chatting to my groom, and sat down with them, when a bullet whizzed by and hit my horse, fortunately

only just scratching him. However, I decided it was
time to be off. Shrapnel was falling about everywhere, and I did not much enjoy the dash from the
gully to Pink Farm. When we got there the silly
groom said he had left his rifle behind, so I had to
wait while he went and got it. Then we started off
again to try and get round by the coast, and rode on
until we got to a little dip in the cliff, where was a
battery of artillery. I asked where the officer was.
We had just had four shells drop very close to us. I
found him in a little deep hole at the end of the telephone. He asked me to come in, and we started to
talk. He said, "Do you happen to know a padre
called Creighton?", and it turned out he was the
——s' nephew, young L——, whom they had told
me about and asked me to look up at Leamington, but
I had not succeeded in discovering him till then. So
we had much to talk about, but the battery chose just
that moment to open fire, and we tried to carry on
conversation while all the time he was receiving directions where and when to fire down the telephone, and
shouting them out to his gunner. It was very
amusing, as I had never seen a battery in action
before. At last there came a lull, and he gave me
some lunch. They fired a tremendous amount while
I was there. I wondered if they were doing any more
damage than the Turkish shells. Then I left the
horses and made my way onto Gully Beach where the
87th Field Ambulance is, but found no chance of
getting up to the regiments. A very deep gully runs
down to Gully Beach, but it was said to be full of
snipers. So I returned, and we got our horses and
rode back along the coast on the top of the cliff. I
stopped to see E—— at "X" beach, and after that on
the way back met crowds of New Zealanders who had

G

just been landed and were going up into reserve.
They were all advancing over a very exposed stretch
in companies. I ventured to expostulate with one
officer I passed. However, he did not seem to bother.
Of course the Turks soon spotted them and started
shelling us, and I saw many of them rushing over the
edge of the cliff as I galloped off to "W" beach. I
believe they had one or two casualties. When I got
back I found the wounded had been largely cleared
off, but decided I had better sleep in another tent, as
the attack was still progressing. I went round the
C.C.S. again, but there was not much to be done.

Saturday, May 8.—H—— is disturbed with the difficulties of life, and the impossibility of doing anything.
So I suggested we should go off together and explore.
We said Mattins, and then started off on foot (I came
to the conclusion a horse was more trouble than it was
worth) along the Krithia road. We got among the
Lancashire Territorial Division and some of the
Artillery and talked to different people, and eventually
started off along the course of a little stream towards
the firing line. We went a good way, but the stray
bullets started again, and it seemed impossible to get
even into the reserve trenches. So we turned back and
found Q——, the L.F. Medical Officer, and had a
chat with him. But H—— felt it was useless going
on, so he returned, and I made my way again to the
gully where I had been the day before. On the way
I met New Zealanders and Australians going up to the
attack, line after line of them. In the gully I found
a New Zealand dressing-station, with a doctor and
padre, and lunched with them. They were very
cheery, but had had a pretty bad time of it on their
own beach. These Colonials are magnificent men.
Again spent bullets made it unwise to go any further.

The attack was to start at 3.30, and to be carried out by the Colonials mainly. So I decided to make my way to Gully Beach, and so up to N——, who, I understood, had his medical station up the gully. I met Corporal M—— on "X" beach, and he led me there. It was a mile and a half up the gully from the beach to him. Stray bullets and shells were whizzing about everywhere, but high up, fortunately, though occasonally they dropped. The Lancs. Territorials were all about, and all kinds of other units in the gully, which became a highway.

At last I found N——, who had a very secure little station on the reverse side of a cliff, and seemed quite happy. The regiment had been having some casualties, and three men had recently been buried without a service. I had some tea. I felt very inclined to go up to the regiment, who were in reserve trenches further up, but Corporal M—— said it would not be safe. Meanwhile the attack was developing, and there was a blaze of artillery. So there seemed nothing for it but to return. I met R—— and C—— and D——, either that day or previously, and they all seemed flourishing. I have heard since that R—— (the Presbyterian chaplain to the Division) greatly distinguished himself in the K.O.S.B. landing. But that is a second-hand story. It was getting dark before I got back. The difficulty is to realize what is going on. As a matter of fact, what happened was that the Australians and New Zealanders made a tremendous charge about 6 p.m. They fixed bayonets, and, with three shouts for Australia with the Brigadier and Brigade-Major in the firing line, they rushed forward in masses against an extremely strong position full of machine guns. They were simply mown down. I have no idea of the actual

casualties, but the Colonials estimate it at somewhere near 1500, out of something like 6000, or
perhaps less. It was simply ghastly. They gained,
I believe, 700 yards. But when I got back to camp
the wounded were already pouring in—those who
could hobble. I never saw a less complaining lot.
They bore their wounds absolutely stoically. "But it
was fine to see the boys charge!" was the one comment. I think the idea of the three days' operations
was to rush Achi Baba by these different attacks. But
the Turks had dug themselves in, and had machine
guns all about, and it was absolutely impossible to
oust them by direct attack : hence these fearful casualties, almost equalling the landing. All regiments
suffered during the three days, but none so badly as
the Colonials.- The facts of the attack are difficult to
gather now, and must be left to a future historian.
But all I can vouch for was the ghastly mass of casualties which came in this night and all Sunday up to
ten o'clock Sunday night.

The 88th Brigade (the 86th had been broken up,
owing to small numbers) were holding the first line of
trenches when the Australians and New Zealanders
came through them to the attack. Every officer and
man I spoke to afterwards said it was one of the most
magnificent sights they had ever seen. On they
dashed, as though nothing could stop them. As those
in front were shot down, others came up from behind
to fill in their places. I had been very anxious to
know what our highly disciplined regulars would say
about the fighting qualities of these men, about whom
the want of discipline, as we understand it, was such
a constant comment. I never heard anything more
about it afterwards from those who saw their charge
that day. There was not a word but of unqualified
admiration.

MACHINE-GUN SECTION OF ROYAL FUSILIERS IN A TRENCH, EARLY IN MAY

As a delightful commentary to this, I have recently heard from a friend, just arrived from Australia, that a wounded Australian officer, who had returned, was speaking to the boys of a large public school. His opening remark was, "Now, boys, I want you to understand that there has never been a finer fighting unit than the 29th Division." The Australian is often accused of having a high opinion of himself. But he certainly knows where and when to praise, and every one of them whom I subsequently met, and who had seen anything of the 29th Division, was unqualified in his admiration for them. Often they would add, "We see now the value of discipline."

Sunday, May 9.—It was impossible to hold services. The camp was fearfully busy, and full of wounded, and my regiments were in the firing line. I went to the C.C.S. and round our own tents, and gave out cigarettes. There was a mass of wounded everywhere. The bad cases had started coming in during the night. They came in all day. Terrible stomach wounds and head wounds. The Australians, who were the vast majority, were wonderfully plucky. I saw the Brigade-Major lying on a stretcher in the open. "My, it was grand to see the boys charge! There was the Brigadier, and he shouted out, 'Now, boys, at them!'" People who saw it said it was a great charge, but utterly reckless. They don't seem to understand fear, and even the wounded were only anxious to get better and have another go! But what a terrible waste it all seemed of such magnificent men! It was a bad day: I believe they cleared off 700 wounded from the C.C.S. that day alone, and still it was full at night again. I decided eventually to go up again and see if I could hold any services anywhere. So I got up to Q——'s station again. He was close to the Australian station, and had had a bad night of it helping them. So had our own dressing-station. Q—— was feeling a little blue. I brought Gospels with me, and sent some up to the firing line. I had lunch with him, and then went over to the Australian dressing-station, and found they still had a large number of bad stretcher cases there, but that the stretchers had given out. So I decided to go back to camp and see if I could raise any more stretchers. But I found it difficult as usual to do anything, and mainly met abuse when I asked. I found H——, and went round with him, but I think everybody was at their tether end. The ships were all full; eighteen cases were taken off, and, after spending two hours going round them in a mine-sweeper they were all returned. However, our Colonel was getting ambulance-wagons to go out as quickly as possible. I think it must have been that day that I discovered oranges were being sold on the beach, and I rushed down and secured a huge basketful, took them round with another man, and gave one to each wounded man, for which they seemed exceedingly grateful. The only services possible were two or three little ones H—— and I took with the less serious cases in the C.C.S. It was a pretty dismal day. Then we found there were some sixty more to come in. We would need every available tent to put them in, as the C.C.S. was so full. The doctors were dead tired. So I sat up to see if I could do anything. We eventually got the sixty, mostly serious cases in great pain, all stowed away. These stomach wounds are terrible. Well, about 11 p.m. everything was finished; only we were expecting more in at one o'clock. So I got up again for these, but found it a false alarm, and only four more cases came in.

Monday, May 10.—The ships were still full, so they could not be cleared from the C.C.S. I counted some thirty-five stomach cases there, three officers. One or two had died. Well, as usual, it did not seem much use hanging round, so I decided to go off and see the Dubsters (Dublins and Munsters joined into one regiment), who, I heard, had come into reserve on Gully Beach. I made my way there, calling on E——, on "X" beach, on the way, and first of all came across the South Wales Borderers, and was hailed by their officers, and lunched with them. They had suffered very heavily (over 100 casualties) in the last attack : fixed bayonets against machine guns. Then I went on to the Dubsters, who had a delightful rest-camp along the beach, and saw O'Hara, and Floyd, and the Munster officers, and arranged an evening service for the few Anglicans. Then I started up the gully to find out news of the R.F.'s, and on the way up was hailed by the cheery voice of J——, who was having tea with an artillery major at the top of the hill, and I joined them. The regiment was just coming into reserve. They had had about 50 casualties (10 killed) since I saw them last. Z—— had been wounded. J—— wanted to insist on my spending the night with them, but I had to return to the Dubsters. However, I went across country in search of the regiment with him before going back, and then came and had a service with the Dubsters, perched on the side of the cliff. I gave them all Gospels, and arranged a Celebration for the next morning. But I had to go back to camp to get my things, so I rode back in time for supper, to find that at last more of the cases had been cleared off, and the Field Ambulance was empty.

Tuesday, May 11.—I had to get up early and ride off with my groom to Gully Beach, where I had a

Celebration on the beach, while K—— held Mass.   I
felt it a little public, but the men were very reverent.
I saw C——, and the South Wales Borderers gave me
some food, and then I rode off in search of the R.F.'s,
whom I found in reserve pretty well in the centre of
the peninsula, with the 88th Brigade.   They were as
cheery as usual, and were planning a trip to "W"
beach, so I asked them to come in, and lunch with the
R.A.M.C. J——, Mundy, and N—— rode in with
me, and the Field Ambulance officers entertained them
all to lunch, which they enjoyed as a change from the
trenches.   We wandered round the beach a bit to see
various people, and I packed up my things to go out
and spend a night or two with them in reserve.   While
doing this I got a note from the L.F.'s, with the sad
news that poor Major Adams had just been shot as
they were getting ready to come out of the trenches.
It was a great blow.   He seemed to have made up his
mind that he was going to be killed, but had been so
much more cheerful when I had seen him the week
before, after having come safely through the first bad
week.   However, the last words he had said to me, as
the regiment returned to the firing line, were, "You
will write to my wife if I get pipped?"   He gave me
her address.   I am glad it was an instantaneous death.
Well, the C.O. asked me to bury him, so I rode back,
the L.F.'s being next the R.F.'s, and found them very
gloomy.   Until then their senior officers were intact,
and he was a very old friend of the regiment, with
about twenty-five years' service.   I sent a note back to
camp, entreating the body to be kept till we came up
at 6 p.m., so that the officers might be present.   The
regiment was sadly diminished, only about 230 men
left in the firing line.   When we got to the cemetery
at six, it was to find he had been buried some hours

before by H——, so I just said a few prayers over the grave, and went with the two majors to see about a piece of ground being railed off to serve as a L.F. burying-place, where some day a memorial might be erected above the beach where they made their famous landing. I came back to supper with the R.F.'s, and slept under a sort of little hedge. Fortunately, I had brought out my oilskin-sheet as well as my ground-sheet, as it rained in the night, and all next morning.

Wednesday, May 12.—It was the first rain we had had since I landed, and was not at all pleasant, as we were in a very clayey field, and everything was in a bad mess. However, I stretched my oilskin alongside a sheet of J——'s, and we made a kind of little tent, where it was possible to keep fairly dry. Fortunately, it was pretty quiet all day and night, and there seemed to be little fighting going on. I went round the lines a little, and the men looked pretty wet and miserable. But we could not complain, as we had had most beautiful weather, and it was not really cold. It was unsettled most of the afternoon, but cleared up enough by 6 p.m. for me to be able to hold a service in an adjoining field for the combined L.F.'s and R.F.'s, to which several officers and a number of men came. But the battle began again just about that time, and raged very fiercely over our heads, a French battery close by opening fire. The whole night was very noisy. I rigged up a little tent with my oilskin, and kept quite dry. It hardly rained, though there was a heavy dew, but the noise of artillery and rifle-fire kept waking me. I don't think anything much happened. The Turks seem to get panicky at intervals, and fire for no particular reason.

Thursday, May 13 (*Ascension Day*).—I had a Celebration at 9 a.m. in the same field, and made it

a commemoration of those who had been killed in the
two regiments, reading out the entire list of names.
Quite a large number of officers and men were present.
I fixed up a little altar, and made it all as nice as possible. The firing had pretty well died down, and we
were fairly peaceful. H—— had a Celebration close
by at the same time for his regiments. It turned out
a lovely day, and the camp soon began to dry up.
K—— came down, and J——, N——, Mundy, and I
rode off with him to lunch at "X" beach. On the
way we saw for the first time our latest pest, a Black
Maria, a lyddite shell fired from a howitzer which has
now got the range of "W" beach. The shells are
most terrifying. They burst with tremendous force
in the air, and blow pieces as far as 150 yards around.
We don't mind the shrapnel much, but these are most
terrifying. They also fired some common shells at us,
and one fell right among a party of men bathing on
"X" beach, but did no damage. After lunch we got
hold of a steam pinnace, and went aboard the *A——*,
where we found M——, and had baths, and then had
tea with the purser in his cabin. They had been
having a tremendous time with wounded, and there
were 1000 of the slighter cases on board. I also saw
a paper of May 4, brought out by a King's Messenger,
with lists of our casualties. Coming on the top of the
huge French lists, with the news of the *Lusitania* and
the *Goliath*, I fear people at home will be feeling
perturbed, and the enemy will rejoice.

We went on board the *Implacable* on the way back,
where I met Ashmead-Bartlett, the official newspaper
correspondent, who was most pessimistic. "The best
thing we could do was to evacuate the place. This
was developing into a major operation, and we had not
the troops for it. Achi Baba was untakable, except

after months of siege warfare." Three Black Marias
had just fallen on "W" beach, and over forty horses
and two men had been killed, besides several badly
wounded. We could see them burst all along from
the *Implacable*. It is a bad thing when one's base is
under fire, and certainly most unpleasant. The
Goliath had been a bad business. It appears a
Turkish torpedo-boat had somehow penetrated the
destroyer-screen. We all felt pretty blue, especially as no one sees how any advance is to be
made after the failure of the Australian attack. We
keep wondering what people at home must think.
To all appearances the whole expedition was hastily
conceived and badly planned. The men are quite
magnificent, all of them. But you cannot make frontal
attacks against modern weapons without being prepared to sacrifice thousands. The only other thing is
some bold stroke, or new landing. However, it is easy
to criticise, and it is an exceedingly difficult undertaking, which we should never have handled. These
feelings do not make it easy for those here. We have
to get the Government out of a muddle, and have no
idea how to do it, and, meanwhile, we are shelled
wherever we go. Well, when we got back to "X"
beach, only my horse was there. The others had all
been killed by a Black Maria in the lines on "W"
beach. So I let Mundy have my horse, and walked
back with J—— in time for supper. We had a nice
quiet, dry night, and all slept peacefully.

One of the most delightful things was the relation-
ship between the R.F.'s and the *Implacable*—their
mother-ship at the landing. I don't suppose either
will ever forget the other, and the officers and men
never tire of telling me how splendidly the officers and
crew of the *Implacable* had looked after them, both

before the landing, and especially afterwards. After the landing had been made good on "X" beach, with practically no casualties, the regiment had advanced well inland, but had not succeeded in joining up with the L.F.'s on their right. The Turks made a tremendous attack that night in overwhelming numbers, and the R.F.'s were forced back to the brow of the cliff, losing very heavily. The officers told me they felt all was up. There was only the sea behind them. The Commander of the *Implacable* thought something was wrong, and, though he had not been instructed to do so, took it on himself to open fire on the oncoming Turks, and did it with such effect as to save the situation.

Friday, May 14.—I spent the whole day quietly in the reserve trenches. The Turks fired a quantity of shells that and the following morning. All the reserve troops were in full view of Achi Baba, and my only wonder is that they did not shell us incessantly. Fortunately for us, the shells went mostly to the right, where the troops were closer. Sometimes eight would come altogether. They mostly burst too high, or did not burst at all, and it is wonderful how little damage they do. I believe only two men were killed and one or two wounded all the time, though hundreds of shells must have burst among them. Of course, these were ordinary shrapnel, and not Black Marias. When they had stopped I wandered over to a little round hill to our right, close to which they had been dropping, to find out the extent of the damage. I found some New Zealanders there, but they had mostly burst further back over the R.N.D. I distributed some New Testaments among the L.F.'s, and found that they had just got orders to move, and were feeling very annoyed, and weary of life. They went off at 4 p.m. that afternoon to join the Indian Brigade on the extreme left of our line, and I promised to go and

ROYAL FUSILIERS HEADQUARTERS' MESS ORDERLIES IN CENTRE OF CAPE HELLES EARLY IN MAY

Note cultivated land.

see them as soon as possible. I got a number of papers of different kinds off them, and that day we spent very quietly, mostly sleeping and eating. In the evening I went over and had a pleasant chat with the Brigadier and Staff—very nice fellows. F—— is acting as Brigade-Major, and doing it very well.

From a letter dated May 14 :—

"I am exceedingly flourishing, the weather is delightful, there are lovely flowers, many birds, heaps of food, plenty to do, and it would be all very jolly if it were not for the war. I wrote a lot of hasty impressions last time, just after having had my first experience of war. Well, since then they are constantly varying. I wonder how much they have let you know in England. One thing is quite clear, and that is this is a far bigger job than they had ever imagined, and fraught with difficulties, some of which appear pretty insurmountable. However, if it were possible to make a landing here at all, it should be possible to go on and do the rest. The main nuisance at the present is that there is not a spot of land in our possession on this peninsula where one is safe from shell fire. Fortunately, the Turkish shell are mainly bad, and do comparatively little damage. They have been bursting all around us all morning, but I know of no one damaged yet. Shells are flying over our heads all the time as I write. They fortunately are directed very high, and no one pays any attention to them. But I find it a little disconcerting. It is terrible how many people we have lost killed. You will have noticed that in the casualty lists. Men who were at Mons say that was nothing to what they have been through here. However, they are all pretty cheerful, the weather being fine, and there being plenty of food. There seems to be a singular callousness as to the value of human life, so many in proportion to the whole force have been killed. (Shells still passing, and no one paying any attention, though somebody must be hit, as the whole place is covered with men and horses.) Well, it is a strange, sad world, and it is no use worrying about anything or wondering what is going to happen, but simply to keep calm, and do the job nearest at hand; still there is absolutely no feeling of security about anything. However, there are many little opportunities of being of use. (There is an aeroplane of ours flying overhead, and they have been shooting at it all morning.) In many ways I am enjoying it all, but it is an awful desperate business."

SPECIAL ORDER

General Headquarters,
May 12, 1915.

For the first time for eighteen days and nights it has been found possible to withdraw the 29th Division from the fire fight. During the whole of that long period of unprecedented strain the Division has held ground or gained it, against the bullets and bayonets of the constantly renewed forces of the foe.

During the whole of that long period they have been illuminating the pages of military history with their blood. The losses have been terrible, but mingling with the deep sorrow for fallen comrades arises a feeling of pride in the invincible spirit which has enabled the survivors to triumph where ordinary troops must inevitably have failed.

I tender to Major-General Hunter-Weston and to his Division at the same time my profoundest sympathy with their losses and my warmest congratulations on their achievement.

Ian Hamilton,
General.

The rest was for five days.

HEADQUARTERS' MESS, ROYAL FUSILIERS, EARLY IN MAY, IN CENTRE OF CAPE HELLES, WITH AUTHOR

CHAPTER VIII

QUIETER DAYS

(May 15—31)

Saturday, May 15.—I stayed in camp all day, writing my diary, except when the Black Marias started and we all rushed down to the beach under shelter of the cliff. Fortunately, though several fell, none did any damage that day. But one feels such a fool cowering under a cliff. I crawled back after a while and visited the C.C.S., which was being emptied. There had been practically no casualties all this week, and very little fighting. In fact " W " beach, the base camp, is now the most dangerous spot. H—— returned at 7.30, and I then went back to the R.F.'s to spend a last night with them. I took two funerals in the afternoon. I also went round to try and arrange about some services in camp, but found it very difficult, as there are so many odd units, and could only leave a notice with the camp adjutant. No Black Marias fell after 1 p.m.

Sunday, May 16.—I was up in good time to get ready for a 7.30 Celebration. Most of the men had been on Ascension Day, so I did not expect a large congregation. I fixed everything up in a field, but the Turks started sending their morning shells, and they were dropping much more in our direction. One fell right in our camp, but did no damage. However, I felt it would be a little unwise to have a service in

the open while they were dropping about, and as no
one came to it packed up again.   After breakfast I said
good-bye to the R.F.'s, who were to go up to the
firing line that afternoon, and walked back to camp
to take a morning service there, while H—— came out
to the brigade.   I met him on the way and said I
hardly thought it wise or safe to hold a service, but he
persisted and held one, fortunately without damage.
C—— had a man wounded at one of his.   I found
L——, the Wesleyan, holding a service when I got
back.   I was to have mine at 10.30.   But just as I
was getting ready the Black Marias started again, and
one burst right in camp, doing no damage, I believe.
By the way, I forgot to say that one burst in one of
our operating tents on Friday and blew it to pieces,
together with a number of stretchers and blankets inside, but fortunately no one was there.   We are all
rather jumpy in camp in consequence, and it is a
singularly uncomfortable feeling.   Everybody rushed
to the beach and took their horses with them, and we
cowered under shelter of the cliffs.   Some more burst
around, but after a while they stopped and we crept
out.   A service by now was out of the question.   So
I decided to go off to "X" beach and see who was
there.   I found the R.F. Transport men sorting letters,
and got two from home which were most acceptable,
but not a newspaper or anything else.   Everybody
else seems to get papers and all kinds of little luxuries.
I lunched with the beach master, a marine, and then
walked on to Gully Beach, where I saw Floyd and
O'Hara of the Dublins, and arranged to come back
later and hold a service if possible.   I heard the
L.F.'s were some way further up on "Y" beach where
the K.O.S.B.'s had made their historic landing, and
which had again been got hold of by the Gurkhas, who

had been doing well on the left. It was a good mile and a half further, along the edge of the cliff. A number of dead horses which had been thrown into the sea had been washed up there and the smell was horrible. Fatigue parties were making a road of sorts. At last I found the L.F.'s next the Gurkhas. They were right on the beach in a very peaceful and secure spot, though only 400 yards from the firing line. You could hear the sharp report of the rifles of one or two snipers going all the time. A very steep path, well made by engineers, leads up the hill to the firing line. They seemed rather more cheerful, and I had a service for them at 4 p.m., most of the officers coming. They asked me to come and spend the night with them. I went back and held a service at 6.30 with the Dubsters high up on the side of the cliff. So I felt my Sunday had not been altogether in vain as I had first feared. I then walked back, meeting C—— on the way and getting in at 8.30 p.m.

Monday, May 17.—I have decided to try and do just what H—— wants, even against my judgment. So I arranged to go out while he stayed in, and to take my turn in on Tuesday. I wanted to spend the night with the L.F.'s, not knowing when I would see them again. I stayed in writing till early lunch, and then got on my horse and rode over by Gully Beach, where I saw C—— and borrowed some books. I managed to ride all the way along the rocky strip of coast. I spent the rest of the day with the L.F.'s, and held a service at 6.30, as so many had been unable to come the night before. It is a delightful spot for a camp, and they were cheering up. For one thing, the first drafts were arriving from England, and each regiment is getting an officer and 46 men. Also 30 wounded men were returning, including Bromley the adjutant.

H

Now they have 10 officers and a grand total of nearly 400 men, and further drafts of 100 men are said to be on their way. So it may be possible to partially reconstitute the Division. One has to be thankful for the smallest mercies. The Inniskillings were in the firing line, and I discovered it was quite safe to go up. Armed with a periscope I clambered up the steep hill, bullets and occasional shells whistling overhead all the time, till I found myself in the support line, out of which leads a little narrow trench, down which I walked a few yards, till I got into another. I asked where the firing line was, and was told that was it. I went a little way to the left, where there was a loophole, but did not look through it much as the snipers were busy, using the periscope instead. I could just make out the line of Turkish trenches, and could see where they had fixed a barbed wire entanglement the night before quite unbeknown to our men, who should never have allowed it. But of course I could not see a Turk. Their line is very strong, and it seems exceedingly difficult to do anything against it. The General had been up shortly before. Snipers were firing all the time, and one or two men had been killed by putting their heads over the parapet. One poor sergeant was even shot through the parapet next morning. He was still alive when I saw him, but quite unconscious. I had always wanted to get into the firing line. I went up again at night and buried a man who had died, in a little cemetery they have fixed on the hill-side. I had to read the service by the light of my electric torch. I feel it is the only consolation one can give the relatives at home. We also consecrate the graves. I spent a good night with the L.F.'s, even having bags of grass to sleep on, and there was very little firing. I had a bathe in the afternoon.

"Y" GULLY WITH GURKHA BLUFF ON THE LEFT, LEADING UP THE
CLIFFS FROM "Y" BEACH. THIS FORMED THE MAIN LINE OF
COMMUNICATION ON THE EXTREME LEFT

Tuesday, May 18.—I went round and tried to talk to some of the men, but found them rather shy, not like the R.F.'s. We breakfasted very late, and immediately after I again climbed the hill and buried another Inniskilling sergeant. It seemed so strange standing only a few yards from the firing line, and hearing the "ping, ping" of the bullets overhead, and burying these poor fellows who had just been killed. Personally I really envy their sudden death, which I cannot help feeling a very merciful thing these perilous days. I feel absolutely no fear of death, but I should hate to be mangled or badly wounded. They started to shell the beach that morning, but could not drop shells close enough, at least while I was there, to do any damage, the hills are too steep. However, they may place their guns in better positions. Then I rode back, getting in at 11.30 to set H—— free. I found more Black Marias had visited the camp in my absence, and three men and several horses had been absolutely blown to pieces and more wounded. It is only one now and then that does damage, but quite enough to make us all feel exceedingly uncomfortable. Being a great coward myself, I got my servant to dig a deep pit in my tent and throw a mound round it, so that I can drop in when they start. It minimises the chances of being hit by a splinter, but if one were to lodge right in the hole or burst overhead it would be an end. However, one must take some risks. While I have been writing this afternoon some more have been bursting on the aerodome just short of camp. I don't think they can realize what damage they are doing, or they would never give us any peace. Personally I would rather be anywhere than on "W" beach. I have been sitting writing in my hole all afternoon. I shall try and construct some overhead cover later on.

At last I have written up to date. It is a nuisance feeling we have embarked on such an utterly foolhardy and under-estimated enterprise. We were to have taken Achi Baba the day we arrived. That is three weeks ago, and it is untaken yet. The Turks have immensely strong positions all up the hill, and quantities of artillery and machine guns manned by Germans. It is another bit of siege warfare. And how are we to do this and carry on the war in France too? The Turkish positions only get stronger every day. We gave them such a lot of warning. They are magnificently led, well armed, and very brave and numerous. Now there are submarine scares and we see the ships in the harbour disappearing. It is all rather dismal. The best things are the weather, which is superb, and the food, which is really excellent. In fact it is like a picnic except for the fighting and the Black Marias. How I hate them! And here we feel we are utterly stuck and nobody seems to know what to do. This was not at all the Government's programme. The Balkan States are not coming in, and I don't blame them. It looks like a question of stalemate and nothing happening. We must advance, but how? The only thing to do seems to be to try and cheer people up as much as possible, and remind them that it is not our fault, and that the whole world is in a pretty good muddle, and we can only each try to do our best. How everybody longs for it to be over! You seem to hear nothing else. But it is a great thing to have fine weather, plenty to eat, no lice, and to feel well. I feel so sure that, though it is impossible to see how, somehow or another some day good will come of the whole war. It always seemed so impossible for the world to go on as it was. And it takes a long time for men to break habits and to learn to care about the things that matter. I cannot pray (though I may long) for victory; only "Thy Kingdom come."

When I had finished writing I wandered off for a little voyage of exploration. The C.C.S. was empty, so I walked all along the edge of the cliff. There were transport horses and mules and wagons of every kind, closely packed in the effort to find cover from Achi Baba and the Black Marias. Then I got to "V" beach and went on board the *River Clyde*, inside of which the Dublins and Munsters had been, which had been run ashore the fatal day of landing. There she had lain ever since, a perpetual mark for the Turkish batteries on the Asiatic side. A pontoon pier had been run out from the shore to her, and most of the troops and horses have been landed on it. The naval lieutenant in command took me over. She has been shelled incessantly and is full of shell-holes, but strangely there have been no casualties among those on board and the very numerous troops that have been landed from her. They had piled up sandbags as protection, and the little saloon under the bridge was untouched. The French use the beach and the old ruined castle, or what of it remains. The Asiatic batteries are a horrid nuisance. I wandered back, looking at the ruined forts and the remains of the labyrinth of barbed wire which the Turks had erected everywhere, and trenches which wound about all over the place. It is almost inconceivable how we ever effected the landing. I came back past Divisional Headquarters, and talked to one or two men, and looked at aeroplanes in the aerodome next to it. I think it is this they keep aiming their Black Marias at. A man asked me if it would not be possible to have a service up there.

Wednesday, May 19.—I started off soon after breakfast and walked a long way—nearly five miles—right

up to the R.F. trenches. I went along the cliffs by
"X" beach, and then cut across into the gully (to
which I have often referred and shall). They have
made a good road down into it. An artillery colonel
walked with me part of the way, and part the chief
engineer. The road drops into the gully, which is
very deep and narrow and goes all the way up the
bed of the stream, winding along through steep banks
covered with scrubby bushes and quantities of flowers.
They are making the road gradually, and it is a regular
highway. All the time the "ping, ping" of bullets
overhead. I am always a little suspicious of the stray
bullets, which have a way of dropping into the gully.
Eventually I came to the Headquarters of the 14th
Sikhs, who are up there with the Gurkhas. The gully
runs almost parallel to the sea, the Indian Brigade, to
which the L.F.'s and Inniskillings have been attached,
holding the line from "Y" beach to the bottom of the
gully.

I next came to the R.F.'s, where I found M—— in
command. They were all a little weary, having been
there three days and nights in the trenches. They had
lost three men killed and a few wounded, but had got
a draft of 46 men with an officer and X—— and some
25 wounded back. To get into the firing line, all that
is necessary is to climb up the side of the gully and
go straight in by a communication trench. The Sikhs
hold a small part, and then come the R.F.'s with just
over 400 yards. They had been working hard improving the trench, and got it into splendid shape wide
enough to walk down. It all wound and twisted
along, with men sleeping in little niches dug under
the forward parapet. They get their water suppy even
up there by sinking tins at places in the bottom and
letting the water slowly rise into them. The General

arrived while I was there, and I went along with him, G——, and X——. We had periscopes, and I could just make out the line of Turkish trenches continuing from where I had seen them before, right across the peninsula. Men were on the look-out at intervals. Sniping was going on all the time and one had to keep down. There was a splendid machine-gun position at the end, and while I was there they saw some Turks digging (though I could not quite see myself), and had a pot at them with the machine gun, till they stopped in a hurry. They seemed quite comfortable in the trench, and quite as secure as we are on "W" beach. It was very interesting.

I came back and lunched with the officers and had a lot of talk with J——. He is a really A1 fellow. The General himself said, "You cannot expect to find J——s on every tree." Our views of life agree very much, and he is much more original than most officers, being a good Liberal and valuing independence and detachment above all things. So we talked a lot. Then I talked with M—— and others, had tea, and then wandered off through the Gurkhas' trenches to "Y" beach and saw the L.F.'s just as they were getting ready to go into the firing line. They have now got ten officers and seem more cheered. It was rather alarming clambering up through the hills and into wired trenches. I got into the wrong ones on my way back and made it much longer. I love the Sikhs. They are so clean and handsome, and have such good teeth. They seem to wash themselves, their hair and beards and cooking-pots in the water in the gully all day. I had some talk with them and their officers, who seem very nice. The Gurkhas, of course, are charming, but I did not have much chance of seeing them. I got back to supper with the R.F.'s

and walked back by the light of the new moon, taking
one and a half hours, and only getting in at 9.30,
being challenged a good deal on the way.

My servant has made the most wonderful dug-out in
my tent. It is just like a grave about three and a half
feet deep, carved away underneath on the side nearest
the enemy. Earth is piled up round the tent both
inside and outside, and half of the dug-out is covered
over in a most ingenious fashion with a covering made
of sandbags and tins full of earth on wooden stakes all
carefully piled up. So I shall not fly any more to the
beach. Chances are reduced to a minimum, and I am
probably safe unless a Black Maria bursts immediately
on top. It is very snug to sleep in. We don't seem
to have had any Black Marias actually the last two
days. The first night I slept in my dug-out I awoke
and could not imagine for the life of me where I was.
I heard the sound of firing, but could not understand
what it was. I have never felt so absolutely lost.
People come and view my dug-out now with envy.

Thursday, May 20.—I stayed in camp all day again
to please H——, and for no other purpose, as there
was nothing for me to do. However, I wrote my diary
and various letters most of the morning and part of the
afternoon. I also wandered off and made a little sketch
of the *River Clyde,* and "V" beach in the evening,
but it was not a success. I had tea with W—— of the
cyclists, and a talk with Y—— of Headquarters; chief
of staff, I believe. I knew his brother in Canada.
The artillery have been short of ammunition lately and
it has been difficult to make any progress. The Turks
do not seem to be short. They kept pouring in shrapnel all over the place all day long, but did not bother
us on the beach, I am glad to say. In fact we have
not had any Black Marias for some days. They seemed

CAPTAIN J——, ACTING C.O., ROYAL FUSILIERS, WITH FIRE TRENCHES JUST VISIBLE BEHIND

to be after the French artillery more than us. So I spent an uneventful but restful day.

Friday, May 21.—I rode off after breakfast up the gully to the R.F.'s with things for the night. As I was riding down the gully who did I suddenly come upon sitting by the side of it but Majors Brandreth and O——, who were both returning cured of wounds received the day of landing. This was a very cheering sight and quite unexpected. They had their packs with them and were very hot and tired. I insisted on their putting their packs on my horse and walking with them. They seemed quite cheerful. Great rejoicings in the regiment to see them back. Nothing had been done and no progress made. It was most important to press the line of trenches forward. Now a solution of all troubles came by Brandreth taking command. He got to work at once and inspected the position and saw the General. It was decided to go out that night. I stayed with them all afternoon. They had succeeded in getting a few men out in pits a few yards in advance of the line. I went down the trenches again. I stayed in the doctor's dug-out that night. Poor L. C. Thomas, who had been church orderly, was shot in the trench, and I buried him at 8.30. Every one went into the trenches and we were prepared for a bad night. Fortunately only four men were wounded that night. The first was hit badly by one of our own shells. I was up several times during the night. Brandreth insisted on going out himself first of all with a string, 150 yards in advance of the trench. Fortunately he was unhurt. The Turks did not seem suspicious. I don't exactly know what happened. Soon after one, when the moon had gone down, M—— took his company out and they started to dig a trench. But he seems to have got suspicious, and ordered them to retire before it was finished, when it was not really necessary, and the trench was only dug about two feet down. Everything possible was done for the wounded men. It began to rain in the morning, but did not go on very long, though things became rather muddy. Brandreth told M—— he would have to go out again next evening.

It was very weird sleeping out there. We were in a dug-out just at the bottom of a steep side of the gully. A little winding path led up to the firing line. The ping of the bullets which flew over our heads re-echoed down the gully. Firing went on all night till dawn.

Saturday, May 22.—The regiment was dismal. The night had been rather a failure. A nice officer, Webb-Bowen, of the Egyptian army, joined it in the course of the day. The men were pretty worn out. I went over to the L.F.'s in the morning. I had to climb through endless trenches, but eventually found P—— in a dug-out on the top of the hill overlooking the sea. Nothing much had happened to the regiment. They were busy digging and improving trenches they were taking over from the Sikhs. I went down and saw B—— and Bromley at the bottom of the hill on the beach. A shell had just dropped there and wounded a man. There is no secure spot. I was trying to arrange a Celebration for next day (Whitsunday). I went back all through the L.F. trenches and saw most of the men, and got back to the gully for lunch. There was a lot of firing that afternoon. It appears the Turks had crawled up the reverse side of the little hill and were occupying the trench the R.F.'s had started to dig the night before. This was only natural. S—— had felt very disgusted, and had crawled out to one of the pits dug in advance of our line. But he had insisted on going on further.

Then a message came down the telephone that he had
been hit in the head. So we were all very alarmed.
The doctor rushed up. Fortunately it turned out to
be only fairly slight. He had crawled on with two
men to try and stop the Turks getting into the trench,
and claimed to have shot five of them, and enjoyed his
day's shooting. Just as he was preparing to return he
was hit apparently by a stone knocked up by a bullet.
The doctor could not say how far his eye had been
injured. We put him in the doctor's dug-out, and he
was quite sensible and dictated a message to the C.O.,
and gave me his mother's address and asked me to
write, and I sat with him a good time until the bearers
came and took him off. I stayed on with the regiment
till evening. They were making careful preparations
for the night attack. It was to begin at 8.30. At the
last moment a message came from the brigade that
the company that was to go out was to expect no
support, as they were afraid of a Turkish counter-
attack, and the main trench must be preserved at all
cost. I had supper and then had to return, as I was
to take a Celebration in camp next morning. I felt
very anxious.

Whitsunday, May 23.—My Celebration was rather a
fiasco. H—— had arranged it. I am afraid no one
in camp knew anything about it. The place was
changed to a tent in the C.C.S. at the last moment.
The result was only three staff officers arrived out of the
whole camp. Many men asked afterwards about services.
I felt rather disgusted, as I should have been with the
R.F.'s. I rode off after breakfast, and, as I feared,
met a procession of stretchers on the way. Almost
the first was poor M—— with a nasty wound in the
thigh from a hand grenade, but quite cheerful. I had
better tell the story as I gathered it. At 8.30 his com-

pany crawled out of the trench. The men seemed to feel it was a counsel of despair. The officers knew they could expect no support. They were to rush the trench they had begun with the bayonet, and then dig themselves properly in. M—— was wounded almost at once. Webb-Bowen was then in command. He had only arrived that day. He was wounded twice slightly, but insisted on carrying on all through the night. Poor Hall, who had come from England with the draft and had only just left Oxford, was wounded and died of wounds shortly after. The men rushed forward magnificently, almost officerless. There was a perfect hail of bullets, and then the Turks started throwing hand grenades, which did most of the damage, making ghastly wounds. The men did not seem to get their tools. In any case it was impossible to stand and dig. They kept it up all night, being told they were to try and hold the trench at all costs. It became perfectly desperate. The rifles jammed. Eventually, just before dawn, J—— was sent out to tell them to retire. He walked three times up and down the line, calling out for any wounded, among a hail of bullets and escaped by a miracle. Every wounded man was carried back. Eighteen men were killed, forty-six wounded, and three officers knocked out (poor Webb-Bowen died next night in the C.C.S. as a result of his wounds.

I arrived just in time to bury Hall. The men's bodies (except three) had not been recovered. It was a miserable business. The service did not come off. Fortunately the regiment was relieved by the Worcesters, who arrived about midday and took over. Captain Nelson of their regiment went into the trench and insisted on looking over the parapet, and was shot in the head. Richardson had had a terrible night

of it with forty-six wounded and ghastly wounds
and was very much overstrained. I rushed up into
the trench to see if I could help get Nelson out, but
I missed my way. However, he was carried out and
his own doctor arrived. I have not heard how he
is getting on since. After lunch the regiment eventually moved off down the gully to the reserve trenches.
The men were dropping with sleep. I went with
them. The reserve trench ran about 1000 yards, and
stray bullets were flying overhead all the time. I
walked the whole way down and back. It was impossible to hold a service, so I decided to go out
next day. The men were glad of a rest. When I
got back I looked into the C.C.S. and saw M——
and Webb-Bowen, but they were asleep. Poor Webb-
Bowen was dead next morning.

The way in which Webb-Bowen acted all through
that night is beyond praise. He was twice slightly
wounded, but refused to return. He had only just
arrived, and did not know the men nor they him. I
sat some time with him before he was carried off. His
only anxiety was for four of his men whom he had been
unable to reach and warn, and he reproached himself
with not having found them. As a matter of fact they
all got back safely.

I learnt afterwards that it was the Sikhs who largely
helped to save the situation. The company of the
R.F.'s was in danger of being surrounded by the
Turks when the Sikhs came out to their support.
They came forward absolutely steadily and quietly in
an unbroken line. The men were enthusiastic about
them. I remember one of them saying to me, "I have
changed my opinion about them niggers since last
night." Practically all the R.F.'s had been with the
regiment in India.

Monday, May 24.—I spent the morning at a

chaplains' meeting. First a Celebration for C. of E., taken by U——, who had just arrived and is to be senior C. of E. chaplain. I gave two of them breakfast afterwards. At ten we had our meeting and fifteen were present. It was quite informal. Who should turn up but Moore, whom I had known in Canada! I knew he was about, but he did not know I was here. He was very cheery, and has had a tremendous series of adventures which I cannot go into here. We had a good meeting, the main object of which was to compare notes and to get to know one another. A fine old Scotch Presbyterian, E——, and an elderly R.C. chaplain have arrived for the base. So things will settle themselves better. We discussed many things and were very amiable, and decided to meet every Monday. Moore lunched with me afterwards, and later on I rode off to hold a service for the R.F.'s, which eventually took place, after a good deal of difficulty owing to their long-drawn-out trench, at 6.30. The men sat under the wall of a ruined house while bullets whistled overhead, and I had to sit all the time too. I arranged a Celebration for the next morning and rode back to camp. We had a good deal of rain in the morning.

Tuesday, May 25.—Rather a depressing day. Submarines, apparently from Germany, are about, and after various excitements have succeeded in sinking the *Triumph* at 12.30 in full view of the coast. We saw all the torpedo-boats rushing up, but do not know how many were rescued. It seems strange having a base under shell fire and lines of communication directly threatened by submarines. The aerodrome was shelled all morning and one aeroplane wrecked. I rode out and held a Celebration at the same place at 10 a.m., but very few came. I think they were prevented by fatigues, etc. Then I rode down to Gully

MEN OF THE 14TH SIKHS IN BIG GULLY

Beach and lunched with the South Wales Borderers, and there was a heavy shower. The Turks were doing a lot of shelling everywhere. Their ammunition seems indeed plentiful. Our batteries may not fire owing to shortage. The Turks drop shells everywhere. I forgot to say that the day before I buried a R.F. He had been shot dead by a spent bullet right in the reserve trench. While taking the funeral one of our shells burst prematurely, and there was a shower of bullets and a man was hit (bruised only) in the leg. I carried on and paid no attention. The Turks were particularly busy this afternoon. They dropped shells indiscriminately over all our reserves. People have the most wonderful escapes, but occasionally some one is hit. I rode back to take poor Webb-Bowen's funeral, but found U—— had just taken it. Later I walked round part of the camp with him to show him various odd units which had had no services, and generally explore and discuss. I also wrote various letters to relations of the dead. I wanted to get news of the *Triumph*, but could not. I explored a road being made at the foot of the cliffs to "X" beach and beyond. There are corps of Egyptians and Greeks doing this.

We make very little progress, there is a continual wastage of men, no reinforcements, and now submarines. What is going to happen next? I wonder what difference Italy's coming in will make.

Wednesday, May 26.—I stayed in camp most of the morning, writing my diary, and at mid-day got a message asking me to go out and take a funeral for the R.F.'s. So off I rode as soon as possible, and found a poor fellow had been shot through the head. There had been a tremendous pour of rain the night before in the gully, though not a drop had fallen on the beach. The water had washed away a good deal of the road they had made up the gully, and the trenches were almost impassable, so they had been walking along the top when this man happened to be hit. I lunched afterwards with the regiment. Eight officers arrived while we were lunching. They had just come from England. It appears K. I. is to be turned into a reserve army, and these men were from it. They seemed good fellows, though rather inexperienced. Later on a draft of 150 men arrived with some very senior sergeants in it. Then news came that one of the Territorial brigades was going to be split up and sent to make up the battalions of the 29th Division. This disgusted them all a good deal. Well, I left them and rode down the gully to the beach and then round to " Y " beach. On the way I stopped to see the Dublins. They are getting new officers. I was talking to the adjutant when he suddenly said to me, "How are all the people at home?" and he turned out to be S——, from Egypt, where his mother and sister are. I was delighted that O'Hara had got the D.S.O. He richly deserves it. Then I went on to the L.F.'s on " Y " beach. They were still in the trenches, but I saw B——, and he told me they were coming out next day for a rest. It was a fairly quiet day on the left, though some shells dropped pretty close to the dug-out which he was using as headquarters. P—— and two others had been lent to one of the Territorial regiments and they were getting a large number to fill up. I arranged to go out and spend a couple of nights with them. I had tea with Q—— and rode back here for supper.

Thursday, May 27.—I was awakened by my servant, who told me the *Majestic* had just been sunk. She sank in ten minutes. I believe about fifty men were drowned in both her and the *Triumph*. She was surrounded by small boats, mine-sweepers, trawlers, etc., at the time, and the torpedo was wonderfully aimed to go right among them and hit her. This was another bit of very bad news. The destroyers rushed about afterwards all over the place, and have been patrolling up and down incessantly since, but it seems impossible to destroy a submarine in such deep water. I did not see the *Majestic* sink, but those who did said it was a most pathetic sight, so close to shore. After breakfast I fitted my saddlebags and rode off with U—— to the gully, taking him right up to the top where the Worcesters had taken over the R.F. trenches. We saw C—— on the way. I left him there and went back to the R.F.'s. The Territorials were all just about to come, and everybody was busy and in rather a bad temper. Then I rode off to the 89th R.A.M.C., who were relieving the 88th and had a dressing-station near the West Krithia road. I had a biscuit for lunch there. They only had one or two wounded. So I rode off and left my horse with the L.F. transport, and walked from there to Gully Beach. I saw the Dublins again and found they were going down to "W" beach. I climbed the hill and saw a New Zealand battery and had some talk with them. I was rather glad I had left my horse, as they started shelling the beach. I made my way round to the L.F.'s and had a cup of tea with the Gurkha officers. I like the colonel. Then the L.F.'s began to come out of the trenches, while the Inniskillings took their place and the Gurkhas the Munsters'. There was a good deal of crowding on the beach while the change was taking place. It was a perfect night with a full moon. The L.F.'s had just got their Territorial contingent. But it is wonderful how soon they settled everything up. There is a capital fellow who always looks after me,

I

Shelley, a South African V.C. who helped save the guns at Colenso, and has quite lived up to his reputation here. He is utterly cool and fearless. He takes great interest in me, and makes me a comfortable bed and looks after me. I supped with B——, Bromley, and Q——, and at last everything sorted itself out and there was quiet. It was a wonderfully peaceful night, and I had a good sleep.

Friday, May 28.—In the morning after breakfast I went with Bromley through some trenches into the gully. On the way I buried an Inniskilling who had been shot getting water. Shaw's company was in the gully. He was very busy getting his Territorials into order. I arranged to come over and hold a service. Then I went down the gully and stopped to lunch with the R.F.'s. I walked down to Gully Beach with J——, and we talked of many things, and then round by the shore to "Y" beach. There I went round and saw the men, and had a service at 5.30. Not very many came but several officers. It was rather a bad place. Shaw was there and took me back to his company afterwards. I first held a funeral service over two men who had been buried immediately behind the firing line, which was being held by the Sikhs. One of the men was Cowley, who had performed at a concert I got up at Nuneaton. I then came back and had a delightful service on the side of a hill, which the whole company of over 200 attended. I was given a most beautiful supper of soup, salmon, fresh beef, and two vegetables, bread and jam and tea, and found Shaw had got his company into splendid order. He is a good officer, very strict with the Territorials. One of the officers escorted me back through the trenches, and I got back about 9 p.m. and had another good night.

Saturday, May 29.—I had another Inniskilling

funeral (the poor fellow had been shot by one of his own men returning from putting up barbed wire), and had a Celebration on the beach, rather nice, with about twenty altogether, at 10 a.m. I then packed up and sent off my things. They suddenly began to drop 6-inch howitzer shells right on the beach. They are terrifying—a huge explosion and pieces flying several hundreds of yards round. They had already been sending other shells which did no damage. They sent several more as I crossed the hill into the gully, but I believe they did no damage. "Y" beach seemed such a secure place. I walked down the gully and lunched with the R.F.'s. They had just got orders to go up to the firing line again, and T—— and Brandreth returned from an exploration of the ——'s trenches, and were very disgusted with them—no communication trenches and impossible to get the wounded out. I waited about and finally went with J—— and T—— over to brigade headquarters, where we had tea with the new Brigadier just arrived from France, and F——. There was a fair amount of shelling going on and I had a little difficulty in getting back, via the Field Ambulance, to where my horse was. I saw U—— when I got in about Sunday services.

Trinity Sunday, May 30.—I helped U—— at a 7 a.m. Celebration in the Post Office tent, as I had had services with my regiments during the week. There were about thirty present. Then I helped him with a service on Divisional Hill at which some of the artillery and others paraded, and I took the Celebration afterwards with about twenty-five present. It was a hot and oppressive day. After lunch I rode off to the R.F.'s. A service was impossible as they were getting ready to go into the trenches, and I sat and listened to all the problems, and was much impressed with the

way young Mundy did adjutant's work and seemed to
think of everything. They had been digging a communication trench all night. Further investigation
had made them only more disgusted with the ——'s
trenches, and I saw a very disagreeable sight. I
crossed an open piece of ground going to look for a
place for the doctor to make a dressing-station in, with
Mundy, and found two corpses which must have been
there some weeks. It was rather a bullet-swept place,
but they might have been buried. We rescued some
shovels on the way back. Brandreth returned from
seeing the General, and I listened to him giving out
orders for taking over the trenches. The regiment has
now increased to over 1000. They had rather a difficult time before them. Then I rode back to Divisional
Hill and held a service, mainly with the Veterinary
Corps, and later went down to the Dubsters, who had
taken up their abode on the beach, and arranged an
extemporized service in a big tent used for slightly
wounded cases who are able to do light work. It was
getting dark, and all the light we had came from
four candles. The tent was filled with all kinds of men
and we had a delightful service. I preached on one
of my favourite subjects, Isaiah's call.

Monday, May 31.—The tragedy of the moment is
that I have lost my servant. He was a good boy. But
the regiment needed him back. I hope to get another,
but at present am without one and find it a great
nuisance. I missed the chaplain's Celebration, which
was held at eight instead of 8.30. Four new chaplains
arrived to-day, among them I——, whom I knew well
at Keble. We had a stupid meeting at which we
decided to have no more general ones, and then had
a C. of E. one, when we discussed what to do with
the new arrivals. Moore took me off to see Chater,

who is now adjutant of a Marine battalion at the age of nineteen, and then took me to lunch with their brigade staff. It was interesting seeing something of the Naval Division. We walked off later to the French lines on the right, and made our way through crowds of Senegalese to Morto Bay on the Dardanelles, where we had a delicious bathe, and talked a lot to an Australian artilleryman. It was very interesting discussing the Colonial point of view. One discusses the whole situation *ad infinitum* with every one one meets. The whole place is full of the wildest rumours. We really know nothing except what we actually see. A leaflet, the *Peninsula Press,* is published every day, which gives only good news. Meanwhile it seems more and more hopeless to take Achi Baba by a frontal attack. Rumours of Italy sending an army corps, Balkan intervention, etc., fly about. It has been a very quiet day. We have no artillery ammunition and seem powerless to advance without. It is getting much hotter. The flies are very bad and the dust terribly thick. However, there is little sickness.

CHAPTER IX

THE BATTLE OF JUNE 4

(*June* 1—9)

Tuesday, June 1.—I have left my diary, as usual, unwritten for a week, and now don't know how to write it. Such terrible things have happened since I last wrote that they seem to have obliterated all else.

There was much talk of the big attack that was to be made all along the line, to be preceded by an artillery bombardment. The R.F.'s had gone up into the firing line on Sunday evening to prepare for the attack. I wandered over to brigade headquarters, partly to see F——, and partly to find the way to their trenches. F—— I found laid up with a broken ankle, the result of a fall. He was carried off later to hospital, and the newly arrived General was deprived of his Brigade-Major. The Battalion C.O.'s were there having a pow-wow, and I waited about till they were gone, seeing Brandreth coming out. Then I had a chat with F——. I told him it was absolutely impossible to take Achi Baba by frontal attack. He said he was quite optimistic, after the wonderful effects of an artillery bombardment. Then I got into the gully and made my way, via a long trench, into the R.F.'s headquarters, where I found Mundy, and had some lunch. He was quite cheerful. They were having lots of digging to do. He took me round to show

me what they had done. There was a perfect
labyrinth of trenches, and I went all through them,
saw J—— in a dug-out, and found a lot of digging
going on. The regiment was very large, with drafts,
and Territorials, and new officers. Brandreth had
been called off to another pow-wow. More trenches
still were to be dug that night. Every one was tired
out. However, it had to be done. Then I rode back
to camp.

Wednesday, June 2.—So far as I remember, I spent
most of the day in the R.F.'s trenches. They had
made wonderful progress in digging, but were pretty
well worn-out. I made a very elaborate tour of the
trenches, and buried various people. Their graves
had to be dug in the side of the trenches. I buried
two in one grave, a New Zealand officer, killed some
three weeks before, in another, and a young Territorial N.C.O., killed while getting some water while
I was there. The whole place is littered with un-
buried dead. Amphlett took me all through his part
of the trenches, rather dangerous in places from enfilade fire. A young officer, one of the new arrivals,
passed me on my way out, and I was told he was
Romanes, from Oxford, but I had no chance to speak
to him.

Thursday, June 3.—I again rode up the gully,
left my horse there, and made my way through the
L.F.'s trenches to "Y" beach. I went all along the
firing line, and had a good look at the Turkish
trenches and barbed wire. I saw Shaw, and chatted
with him, and had some lunch with B—— in his dug-
out. Cunliffe returned from the Territorials while I
was there. I went back eventually through the support trenches to the gully, and went over to see the
R.F.'s from there. I was feeling a little upset, had

slept a good deal during the afternoon, and had rather a headache, so I did not go into the trenches, but had supper with Brandreth and Mundy (whom I have never seen again). They got a message while I was there to say they were to be ready for the attack the next day. They had had a little rest that day, and there was to be no digging that night.

Friday, June 4.—I got a note from H——, saying I was in no case to go beyond the first field dressing-station of the Field Ambulance. Otherwise I think should have gone up to the R.F.'s dressing-station. A—— and I decided to change ambulances, as my men would go to the 88th, and his to the 89th. We started off together just before the bombardment. I suppose the whole thing will go down to history, so I need not dwell on it unnecessarily. At 11 a.m. the artillery started to fire for a quarter of an hour, then paused for another quarter, when the troops in the trenches were supposed to shout and wave bayonets so as to get the Turks into the firing line, then another half-hour's bombardment. All we could see was a line of smoke and dust all across the peninsula where the Turkish trenches were, as the shells fell incessantly all along the line. These things have been often described. Certainly it seemed as though a Turk could not be left alive anywhere. Then at twelve it stopped (or was supposed to), and the rifle and machine-gun fire took its place. We were in a dug-out near the Pink Farm, and bullets began to drop round us, one dropping onto A——'s boot, so we decided to retire, and had some lunch at the 89th dressing-station. Some bullets even got as far as there. The battle raged all afternoon. I could make nothing out even with glasses. I waited for some time, but no wounded seemed to come in. It was impossible for them to come over the open among the hail of bullets that fell. So I made my way down to Gully Beach with R——, who happened to come along. There we found the slight cases beginning to come in in crowds to the 87th Field Ambulance. I saw several of the R.F.'s, and gathered they were advancing. But I had learnt before that it is impossible to get accurate news from the wounded. They are naturally a little over-wrought, and only know just the part where they happen to be. We waited round a little, and then started up the gully. The gully was in a perfect turmoil, of course, guns going off on all sides, and the crack of the bullets tremendously loud. They swept down the gully, and one or two men were hit. I cannot imagine anything much more blood-curdling than to go up the gully for the first time while a fierce battle is raging. You cannot see a gun anywhere, or know where the noise is coming from. At the head of the gully you simply go up the side right into the trenches. You see nothing except men passing to and fro at the bottom, and there is the incessant din overhead. Well, I went on up to the 88th dressing-station, two thirds of the way up, and found them very busy. More R.F.'s there. I went right up to the head of the gully to an advanced post of the 87th, and found that the R.F. dressing-station had gone right up to their support trenches, where H—— had been so emphatic I was not to go. I am quite sure it is just the place I should have been. So I returned to the 88th, and asked if I might stay the night, as L.F.'s as well as R.F.'s were coming in. I found S——, one of the new officers, slightly wounded in the arm. A terrible battle was going on. Several officers killed; J—— and others wounded. However, I found it impossible to gather much from him. The doctors gave me some supper in a very secreted sort of hollow in the side of the gully, and after I had been around and seen all the wounded, and no more seemed to be coming in, I rolled up in a blanket, and had a good sleep despite the ceaseless hail of bullets. I was up about 4 a.m., and went down, to find J—— rather badly wounded through the thigh, and in a good deal of pain, but very cheery. I was with him on and off most of the morning, till they took him away. I was really rather glad he was as bad as he was, as it gave some hope that he might survive the war. A large number of wounded had come in, and the wagons came up all morning to clear them.

Saturday, June 5.—Later I went down to Gully Beach and found C——. The place was very full of wounded, who were being got off on boats as quickly as possible. I was feeling very weary, so I lay down in C——'s dug-out, and slept most of the morning. Then I walked round along the coast to "Y" beach to see the L.F.'s. Everywhere, of course, I was hearing about the battle. The left had been held up, unable to advance. The centre had advanced. The casualties very heavy. I found B—— and Bromley. Clayton and Cunliffe had been killed, Shaw was missing. Three companies had gone out, and the total casualties were 450. They had just had a large draft of officers, and twenty-five officer casualties altogether. I saw some of them on the beach waiting to be moved. Later on I walked through the firing line with B—— and Bromley. The whole situation was terrible—no advance, and nothing but casualties, and the worst was that the wounded had not been got back, but lay between ours and the Turks' firing line. It was impossible to get at some of them. The men said they

could see them move. The firing went on without
ceasing. I saw the General, and he said the Sikhs
had lost even more, all their officers gone, and only
180 men left. The 5th Gurkhas, who had just arrived,
had had heavy losses. And all this with no gain
whatever. He took it quite philosophically. No news
of dear old Shaw. It appeared the artillery had not
done the damage to the enemy they were supposed
to do, and the moment the advance started their
machine guns played along the top of the parapet,
and not a man got even up to the enemy's trenches
on the left. The General had suggested putting up
a white flag, and some one going out to the wounded.
They tried this later, but it failed. I buried eighteen
of them in one grave while I was there. Several had
been killed by our own shells, including Shelley, the
South African V.C. The majority of the bodies are
still lying out there. In the gully I buried four more
who had died of wounds. I walked back to "W"
beach, feeling very sad.

I have known few officers who took such care of their
men as Shaw. He was very strict and exact. But
he seemed to neglect nothing. His C.O. said he felt
he could leave him absolutely alone, and knew no one
on whom he could more implicitly rely. He was a
splendid soldier, and quite tireless. He led his men
out that day in perfect order, and I have heard no
more of him since, except a report from one of the
men that he saw him fall.

Clayton and Cunliffe were two other first-rate company commanders. In fact, I was always tremendously impressed with the careful, quiet way the
L.F. officers did their work.

Sunday, June 6.—I was awakened very early by the
sound of furious fighting. It had gone on ever since

Friday midday, but now was intensified. At 7 a.m.
I went to a Celebration, and then off to the 89th dressing-station on the West Krithia road. Nothing happened all day. I did a good deal of digging, as shells
were dropping around, and they had no very secure
place for wounded. I wandered off, and saw E——,
the R.F. Quartermaster. I don't think he had had
news by then of the morning's battle. I forget when
I heard. The Turks counter-attacked early Sunday
morning, about 3.30. Dear Major Brandreth, hearing the firing on his left, went off to see what was happening. He was last seen calling to the ——'s and
——'s, who were breaking, to come on. Two men
say they saw him hit in the neck. Mundy went off at
the same time, and I can get no news of him. T——
was hit, but got away. This left only G—— of the
original officers, and all the ones who had since joined
were gone. I forgot to say that the day before I had
seen young Romanes carried down to the dressing-
station with a shrapnel wound in the head—no chance
of recovery, I fear. He was quite unconscious. I
hung round the rest of the day, dodging shrapnel, had
a nice service in the evening with some Engineers who
had been on the A—— with me, and then came back
to camp.

Major Brandreth, who was in command of the
Royal Fusiliers at the time, and was presumably killed
on the morning of June 6, was greatly beloved by
the regiment which he led so gallantly. He had been
wounded at the landing, but when he returned at once
threw himself with remarkable energy and devotion
into the tremendously difficult task that lay before the
regiment. He was, in my opinion, a type of the
perfect English gentleman, unfailingly courteous to
every one, heedless of danger, indefatigable in his

2ND LIEUT. G—— AND LIEUT. MUNDY, ACTING ADJUTANT, KILLED JUNE 6

work, and possessed of an absolutely simple, straight-forward character. The men and officers all loved him. Personally, I think I felt his loss more keenly than anything.

Several officers were killed on June 4, but I had been unable to get to know them all. They had recently arrived from England, and were the first of the new officers to join the R.F.'s. They certainly were a splendid sample of what the new armies could produce. I can only single out two for special mention. Captain Amphlett assumed command of one company. One of the officers under him had been with the regiment many years, having been regimental Quartermaster-Sergeant. As he lay seriously wounded afterwards he said to me, "I never wish to serve under a better officer than Captain Amphlett." I remember him taking me round his section of the trenches, a very dangerous one, and showing me all the work he had done to improve them and construct overhead cover, etc., where necessary. He seemed to make himself one with his men, and worked ceaselessly for them. They soon got to know him and value his character. He was killed shortly after the attack commenced.

Captain Jenkinson's death was, I believe, described later in *The Times* as one of the greatest losses to science since the war began. He stood quite alone in England, if not the world, in his own subject, Embryology, and had recently embarked on a course of highly specialized investigation in that subject, in which he was a pioneer. I later met some officers who told me that their hope, when at Oxford, had been that when they had taken their degrees in science, they might be able to attend his lectures. He had such a quiet, modest nature that I fear none of us at the time realized his reputation. He had recently been gazetted captain, but said nothing about it, pre-ferring to act as a lieutenant. His letters show what a keen student of Nature he was while on the pen-insula, and how the historical surroundings of the place appealed to him. Strangely enough, the three other pioneers in Embryology have all died within six months of his death.

Monday, June 7.—Our usual chaplains' meeting in the morning was hardly successful: only H——, U——, and A—— there. We decided to try and get a tent for daily services, and to get U—— more definitely attached to the C.C.S. I was longing for news of the R.F.'s, but they had not come out of the trenches yet. The battle had been raging pretty incessantly. I cannot remember what I did that afternoon. I think I went to the 89th station on the West Krithia road, where very little was doing. The 86th Brigade was to be reconstituted, with Y—— as Brigadier. The R.F.'s would be out of the trenches that night. I discovered X—— in the hospital, with a bad wound in the stomach. He was taking it very well. He had been hit on Friday soon after the advance, but had been got back into the trench, where he lay for twenty-six hours. He said he could not imagine that pain could have been so great, or an experience so awful. The battle raged all the time, and he did not know if the Turks would retake the trench. Of course lying still was the best thing for his wound. He lay in hospital several days, and seemed to be doing well when they took him off. He said his verse for the day happened to be, "I reckon that the sufferings of this present world cannot be compared to the glory that shall be revealed," and that the words had helped him to bear up more than anything else.

From a letter dated June 7:—
"A very terrible battle has been raging the last three

days. I must not say anything about it, but I think, either killed or wounded, I have lost every friend in my special regiment. I have not been able to see them yet, but hope to this morning. I must not give any numbers or facts. I suppose everybody in England now is beginning to realize what war means. The lists from France are terrible. It is absolutely inevitable they should be so in trench warfare. To win a victory is practically an impossibility, and there can be nothing but a deadlock, and endless slaughter. I see these young fellows come out from England full of patriotism. They go straight into the trenches, and are killed in a day or two. At least this is the result of my observations. Meanwhile, I have a job in which it is part of my duty to protect myself and keep out of danger. It seems so unreasonable that certain people should have such jobs. I have to sit in safety while my regiments go into action, and my friends are lying untended between the trenches. And yet we must not be overwhelmed by the misery and sufferings of war. I feel so absolutely certain that these men will find their reward in ways they never before dreamt of. Their sufferings will be their blessing. I am so glad you say people in England are brave about it all. We think a lot about them. I don't think anything worries a soldier so much as thinking others are worrying over him. Of course they cannot help it, but their bravery will help him. Everybody does hate it all so terribly. I think it is better they should. It would be rather terrible if they liked it—so unnatural. One so easily becomes faithless and says, "To what purpose is this waste?" But there must be a great underlying purpose, and men who feel it all must turn to God, and leave it with Him. The battle never stops, and there is no spot free from shell fire. They started shelling the beach last night from the Asiatic side after we were all asleep; but fortunately they did no damage, though one shell spluttered earth onto my tent. But one gets quite cunning at avoiding shells. Only they have a stupid way of dropping them at any moment on any spot, quite at haphazard. And no place within two miles of the firing line is free from stray bullets, which drop into the most unaccountable places, and occasionally hit a man. However, these are little risks that cannot be avoided."

Tuesday, June 8.—I went to Gully Beach, where I found what was left of the R.F.'s, and stayed with them till Friday. It was so tragic. I came out with such a magnificent regiment, with such regimental pride, and such a united and delightful band of officers. Only one left, G——, the former Sergeant-Major, besides the Quartermaster. He was asleep when I arrived. There were Corporal M——, and the other officers' mess orderlies—but no mess. The regiment had dug incessantly for five days, and then fought incessantly for three days. They had lost five out of the six remaining officers, all the ten officers who had recently joined them, and somewhere about 200 of the remaining men. Of the original regiment, including transport, stretcher-bearers, etc., 140 were left. The Sergeant-Major was still there, and seemed all right, but had to knock off work for three days. G—— was quite played out. I made every possible inquiry during the following days after Brandreth and Mundy. Two men said they saw Brandreth hit in the neck; one said he saw his orderly—since missing—bandage him up. But no one had seen his body. Mundy was quite lost sight of. Were they wounded prisoners? Not likely, but just possible. The men were wonderfully cheery. They take things very calmly, and were glad to be on the beach, where they could get plenty to eat, and plenty of sleep in perfect peace and bathe as often as they liked. Corporal M—— gave me some supper, and we tried to pretend it was the same mess. A scout party went out that night to try and discover the bodies of the dead, but could do nothing owing to the heavy fire. Dear old Brandreth, it is too terribly tragic. I would give anything to know where he is. And Mundy, too. I am only glad that J—— has got a sufficiently serious wound to keep him away from it all for a good while. I collected the regiment in the evening, and spoke to them and tried to cheer them up. I slept with G—— in his dug-out, and tried to cheer him up. E——, the Quartermaster, appeared, and was very cheery.

Wednesday, June 9.—I stayed on at Gully Beach with the R.F.'s. I wanted to look after the mess, and help keep them going if possible. A Captain Taylor, of the Dublins, arrived to take command. He was followed by a number of officers from different regiments. A draft also arrived in driblets—altogether about 200 men, making the grand total up to nearly 500. The new officers were all strange to each other and the regiment. I believe there are about fifteen of them now. I find it difficult to get to know them. There was absolutely none of the old regimental feeling left. I slept with one of the new arrivals that night and the following. The mess swelled to large numbers, and we were always having visitors. The 88th Brigade were relieved, and I awoke to find the Hants streaming down. They only had 100 odd fighting men left, and no officers; so there was one regiment worse than ours.

K

CHAPTER X

(*June* 10—27)

Thursday, June 10.—I awoke to find the Munsters had streamed down on the top of us. They had been with the Dublins in some reserve trenches on the top and had had a tremendous shelling. The L.F.'s had also come down during the night. I had been with them the day before. The officers had a most beautiful and commodious dug-out. The Brigade Headquarters were close by. But the Turks dropped three 9'2 Black Marias among them that evening, killed an R.F., wounded three who were on guard and several other men, including a young Munster officer just attached to the staff who later died of his wounds. So everybody made for the beach that night, and there was a scene of the most tremendous confusion and crowd. I saw the L.F.'s several times before they moved. P—— had had a lot of fever and looked very pulled down. Bromley seemed to be keeping everything going. Despite their enormous losses they still had over 500 left as they had had a very big draft, and there seem to be plenty of officers about. B—— was very played out too. He has now gone off to Imbros for a rest, and P—— has gone as well. I spent my time wandering about among the regiments and seeing all kinds of people. The gully has become practically the base for the 29th Division. The Divisional Headquarters are there now, and General De Lisle has just arrived as Divisional General. The Reserve brigades are put on the beach and in the gully now. Stray bullets are very bad. They drop at a tremendously sharp angle, and men may be hit anywhere, and occasionally are. It makes it feel a little uncomfortable. At night when the firing is heavier, we used to hear them drop into the water. But the beach is practically safe from shell fire.

Friday, June 11.—I stayed on till late evening, going up the gully a bit, bathing with the L.F.'s, and holding two services, one for the R.F.'s in the middle of the crowded beach, and one with the L.F.'s up a little quiet gully. All the end of the week we had very bad wind which blew the sand about everywhere, and made things very disagreeable and people rather snappy. The first regiments of the new Lowland Division had arrived. It seems so terrible taking these boys and making them attack a position like Achi Baba. They put them almost straight into the firing line so as to rest the poor 88th Brigade, but could only keep them there three days. The Turks went on shelling all day, so that the battle which had begun the previous Friday may be said only to have died down that night. The feeling of strangeness in the R.F's did not wear off, and of course the new arrivals were feeling a little gloomy. In fact it has been exceedingly difficult recovering from the effects of the last battle. The Division now is practically unrecognizable, despite the drafts. I think the South Wales Borderers have the largest number of original officers left—eight. Of course it is no use brooding over it, or worrying about those who have been killed, or the fact that we did not succeed on Friday. This is war, and one must harden one's heart and live in hope.   But one lives in a curious sense of insecurity.   There is not a spot on this part of the peninsula which is in our hands that is free from shell fire.   Most of it is within range of the bullets.   And submarines are continually prowling about, cutting off our shipping or sinking our men-of-war.   They don't seem to bother over small supply boats, which still lie anchored off "W" beach quite calmly.   I got in about 9 p.m. that night, and just as I was going off to sleep they started dropping Black Marias close to us, a very alarming experience at night. They did not actually fall in our camp and I think did no damage, but their explosion at night is terrific. They came across the water from Asia.   The original Asiatic Annie only fired small common shells, which did little damage.   She fired at a supply boat for some time next morning, but did not hit it.   But we don't like her new friend.   Shell fire is curious.   It only occasionally does any damage, and then quite unexpectedly.   I think I felt more terrified as I lay in my dug-out that night than at any other time.

Saturday, June 12.—I have been having a good deal of trouble about my batman which I need not go into in detail.   The A.S.C. had at last sent me one, but he knew nothing about horses, and consequently was rather miserable and asked to be returned.   So I had to let him go, though he was a good boy.   Now I hope to get one of the Field Ambulance men whom I had before, which will be much better.   I spent part of the morning discussing things with U—— and H——, and sat a good deal writing in the tent while the wind raged and the sand was intolerable.   I took a funeral in the middle and the sand simply stung my face. The wind delayed the landing of troops and stopped the aeroplanes.   I walked off to the gully in the after-

LOOKING UP GULLY RAVINE. THIS WAS THE MAIN LINE OF
COMMUNICATION ON THE LEFT CENTRE

GULLY BEACH AT THE MOUTH OF GULLY RAVINE

The Headquarters of the 29th were eventually established on the right foreground. Tents
of the 87th Field Ambulance in the distance.

noon and had tea with the 10th Battery, where young
L—— is, and arranged a Celebration at the White
House, the end of the support trenches in which the
R.F.'s are. I also looked in on the brigade officers
who now have moved into the gully, and I gave out
the service to various units. It was a wonderfully
peaceful day—very little firing of any kind.

Sunday, June 13.—I had a heavy day. First a Celebration at 7 a.m. on "W" beach. Then I walked into
the gully and had another Celebration at 10 a.m., at
the White House, to which not many came. Later a
parade service for the 460th Howitzer Battery, which I
enjoyed much. The Major is a delightful man. He
was in France, and is very happy here, and has four delightful young officers under him whom he has trained.
I think they must be Territorials. I had a very pleasant lunch there. The wind was less violent and there
was very little firing again. I walked to the head of
the gully and had a little service for the Munsters,
then back to Headquarters of 86th Brigade and had
an evening service there. I so much prefer these little
open-air services. I walked back here, and felt pretty
dead when I got in.

*Monday, June 14, and Tuesday, June 15, mixed
up.*—The advanced dressing-station of the 89th Field
Ambulance was to move up to the top, or near the top,
of the big gully. So I decided to go with them, especially as my brigade was up in the firing line. I had a
boy in the ambulance given me as a servant, a much
more satisfactory arrangement. So I sent him up in
a wagon with my things. We had a little clerical
meeting that morning. C—— has gone sick with
dysentery. It is getting rather prevalent, and most of
our insides are more or less upset. At the meeting I
heard A.B.—— of Jerusalem and late of Smyrna had

just arrived as chaplain to the newly arrived Lowland Division. So I decided to ride over that way and try and see him. Their camp is about a mile from "W" beach. They are all dug in as every one has to be now. I inquired of a Presbyterian chaplain who pointed out where he was, and as I was riding over to the place, suddenly, without any warning, a Black Maria from Asia dropped just about ten or fifteen yards immediately in the direction I was riding and made a terrific explosion, throwing bits of earth out of a hole about ten feet across and four and a half feet deep for a tremendous distance around. My horse turned at once and bolted, and for quite an appreciable time afterwards pieces kept dropping all round us. I assure you I did not check him, and postponed my visit to A.B.—— A few seconds later and I should not be writing now. Another dropped about 200 yards from me, and I made off for the gully as quickly as I could. They have been strewing them indiscriminately all over the peninsula. They are extraordinarily alarming, but only occasionally do any damage, and then usually to horses and mules, which have been slain in quantities, poor things. However, they at any rate have the advantage of being shot if badly wounded.

One day during the week they dropped 150 shells on "W" beach, half of them Black Marias. I only know of two men actually killed, but every one was tremendously alarmed. I wonder if people at home realize that we are fighting under these conditions. You cannot get out of danger. You cannot rest a regiment without a few men getting hit every day by stray bullets or shrapnel. Of course some places are better than others, but none are absolutely immune. It is a wonder to me how calmly every one takes the situation. Then added to all this we hear the Turks

are bringing up twelve 10-inch howitzers and that che-
mists have arrived in Constantinople to make artificial
gas, and we have all been provided with respirators.
It is impossible to advance more than a few yards at
a time and that at enormous cost. However, we hear
that two divisions of Kitchener's Army are on their
way, which is excellent news if true.

Do people realize our conditions, I wonder, in England? I don't quite see why we should be the only
people who do. If we are wrong we will gladly be
corrected. It seems so unfair that the people who have
to do the thing have absolutely no say in the planning,
and further, that they should be volunteers for the purpose. The German idea is perfectly intelligible. One
is taught from the earliest that one exists for the State,
and that the State has absolute right to control all its
citizens. It says "Go here," and you go without asking a question. We say that the State exists for the
interest of its citizens to serve them, and that England
is a free country. The voluntary system seems absolutely incompatible with war neither initiated nor con-
trolled by the people. I have just read these pages to
one of our doctors and asked him if he considers it a
truthful statement of fact, and he says absolutely, only
perhaps I am inclined to be a little pessimistic. I have
no desire to be pessimistic, only truthful, and I hate a
false optimism which tries to pretend that everything
is going well when secretly one feels very doubtful.
The men are marvellous—even now in the 29th Division, which must have lost as many men and more
officers than it started with. I think if facts were absolutely clearly faced at home we are still wise and great
enough to find a solution. The whole nation—not merely
volunteers—will have to back us up. One sees so
many things one did not see before. Personally I have

absolute faith in our capacity as an Empire to bring everything to a successful conclusion. I am not at all pessimistic there. It is only our inconceivable stupidity and muddle and incompetence. Why should not every single person in the Empire take their own share, and do or give whatever is asked of them? It would make it much easier for everybody. We only want to feel that we are all doing our part and putting forth our best energies. Only we must all be told the plain facts and needs, and realize all the difficulties and look forward a little. This would save us from panic and worry and every one would feel perfectly calm. I think the Colonies are teaching us a great lesson. The spirit of the Australians and New Zealanders here is beyond all praise. Well, perhaps I am only saying what people generally are thinking, and if so it will all come right, and the needless sacrifices we have made will not be so needless as they appear. Perhaps even those in high positions will learn. I still feel it is all so good for us. So why am I a pessimist?

Well, to resume. I rode up to the dressing-station, which I must describe. It is about 500 yards from the firing line in a little gully called Aberdeen Gully (as the 89th come from there), which runs off from the big gully. A narrow path about fifty yards long had been cut out of the bed formed by a stream, now dry. The path runs up into a little natural amphitheatre in the cliff, about fifteen yards in diameter. The sides of the gully are almost precipitous, but it has been widened enough at places to make a dressing-station, cook-house, and officers' mess, and the amphitheatre is also used as a dressing-station if necessary. It is almost absolutely safe, but bullets have a way of dropping anywhere, and a man got one in his arm last

night, and one was at the foot of my dug-out this
morning. My dug-out is reached by a little flight of
steps partly cut out of the soft rock and partly made
of sandbags. It is only just large enough for me,
and is cut into the rock with a piece of corrugated iron
as cover. It is very snug and away from people, and
I sleep on pine branches. There is a mountain battery
close by which they shell a good deal, and pieces come
flying over us at times. It is pretty noisy, as everything re-echoes in the gully, and always at dusk the
Turks start to fire and bullets whirr overhead incessantly. When a battle is on there is a good deal of
shrapnel bursting all around, and it is rather alarming;
but the bullets are really the most dangerous. I spent
the day mostly in preparing my dug-out and fixing
things up generally, but slept in the theatre that night.
I had a very nice little service with the Munsters, who
were in the reserve trenches, and arranged for a Celebration the next morning in the theatre. I found an
officer who was very keen to have one. But they had
a little battle next morning (*Wednesday, June* 16), and
the Munsters had to be called to arms. The Dublins
were attacked in a curious trench, which we share with
the Turks, with a barricade between. The Turks came
out and threw hand-grenades at them, and they had
about 50 casualties (10 killed), but claimed to have killed
about 200 Turks. This meant that the Celebration I
had arranged was upset and only one officer appeared.
However, we had one together. I had been all through
the trenches the day before, and it was interesting to
see the trenches which the Turks had dug and which
we now occupy. The L.F.'s were in them. Bromley
is now both C.O. and Adjutant, and seems very much
to enjoy it. I think B——, who has gone away for a
rest, was getting a little played out, and Bromley finds

it easier to be adjutant to himself. P—— had also gone sick with malaria.

That and the following days I spent around the gully, and did not go away farther than down to the beach. We opened the station for patients on Wednesday and the 87th cleared off, and we have been handling practically all the patients since. There are only a few, except when there is an actual battle. I took the opportunity of being here to do some writing, and hoped I would have plenty of time, but it is surprising how it goes. Just above us a mule-track leads over the hill down to "Y" beach on the other side, where the Indian Brigade is holding the line between us and the sea. I often go up to the top to a place where the artillery have an observation station, and it is possible to see the whole peninsula behind and the maze of trenches in front, and watch any artillery work that may be on, and look all over the sea and see what ships are about. They often drop shells round us, as there is a mountain battery close by which draws a lot of fire.

On Friday (*June* 18) I went down to Gully Beach. The 86th Brigade had been relieved on Thursday morning by the 87th, and were in camp on the beach. I wanted to see if there would be any opportunity for holding services. I saw the Dublins and Munsters camping in the gully on the way. The L.F.'s and R.F.'s were next door on the cliffs. They were to be inspected by Brigadier Y——, so I arranged a little service immediately after in between their lines, and we had a very nice little gathering on the beach. The R.F.'s seem such a strange regiment now that I have seen very little of them lately. I don't find the officers so friendly, of course they hardly know each other, and it is impossible for them to have any corporate feeling. C.D.——, who came out with the last draft, is now C.O. W——— of the cyclists has also joined them. The other officers are just a scratch lot got together anyhow. I feel more at home with the L.F.'s, as Bromley is still C.O. I went to hold a service with the Dublins and Munsters afterwards, but they did not come. A battle was just beginning, and we could hear the Turks giving our trenches at the top of the gully a violent bombardment, and soon bullets began to hail down. It started about 6.30. No one was expecting anything. A lot of the shells came farther down the gully. I started to go up to the dressing-station, but the bullets were getting very thick and I turned into a dug-out on the side of the road. One or two struck the road close to me. Then I saw an ambulance wagon pass and got into it. Close to the White House we found every one cowering in their dug-outs, and they shouted to us to gallop. A mounted orderly came tearing up to us and said, "For God's sake gallop." They had just been shelling that bit of the road heavily, so we galloped, and the wagon swayed from side to side. It was quite exciting. Several horses had been killed. At last we got up to the dressing-station, but the wagon took cover for a bit before leaving with the few patients we had.

The battle continued all night, and the firing was very heavy. The wounded started to come in pretty soon, slight cases as usual first. I decided to stay up with the doctors. There is little one can do, except distribute cigarettes and say a word or two to the men. They came pouring in all through the night. They had had a tremendous shelling over the dressing-station, as evidently they imagined we had reserves in the mule-track trench just above it. Major Archibald of the engineers was hit up there and Davidson went off to see him, but he was too bad to be moved. As the night went on we got more and more filled up until every place was taken. We had to send up to "W" beach for another bearer party, which arrived about 2.30 a.m. under Maurice, and got safely through the bullets. We were really wonderfully fortunate in having no casualties among the bearers, who were continually going up to the regimental dressing-stations for cases, with bullets flying about everywhere. The cases were very nasty—a number of them caused by hand-grenades. We had over a hundred in that night and the next morning. There were two officers of the South Wales Borderers. One died after they had taken him away, I heard. I sat and talked a good deal with another officer, a nice fellow, with a painful but not dangerous wound. Fortunately the 88th next door were able to open up, else we could hardly have taken in every one.

The battle went on, on and off, next day (*Saturday, June* 19). It was all over the trench we share with the Turks, where the Dublins had had their little fight. Farther down the line the ——s broke and the Royal Scots and some Worcesters had to go to their help and retake a trench. Altogether I know of about 200 casualties, mostly South Wales Borderers and Inniskillings. I had a good many funerals to take that morning, among them Cass, an officer. They said that heaps of Turks had been killed, if that is any consolation, and that they had managed to retake everything. It was rather a nasty little battle, but nothing compared to June 4. I went down the gully in the afternoon to arrange services for Sunday. We cleared all the wounded pretty quick and it was practically empty when I got back.

Sunday, June 20.—I had no Celebration myself, but rode down to the beach, where I—— has a tent now close to the new Divisional Quarters, where a Celebration for every one is held. I breakfasted after with the L.F.'s and then had a parade for them on the beach, the first formal parade I have had—quite a large crowd. The Brigadier came halfway through. Then I had a smaller parade with the R.F.'s next door, and afterwards climbed the cliff to the 460th Battery and had a nice service with them, lunching with the officers after it. They are extremely pleasant. Batteries always are. They do not have many casualties and are able to keep their identity, and don't have a very hard life or much strain, and are consequently very cheerful. Then I walked all along the top of the cliff to other batteries, and eventually returned to the New Zealand Battery and had a service there, and then came back and had one here in the theatre for the ambulance men and some others. It makes a splendid place, being absolutely closed in. So I had a fairly heavy day.

Monday, June 21.—I rode off to "W" beach for the chaplains' meeting, to which only a few turned up, and lunched with the Field Ambulance. Then I rode back by the cliffs and found A.B.—— at the 1st Field Ambulance. He was in great form, full of energy and quite happy, and it was nice seeing him again and talking over things of years ago now. Then I saw F—— on Gully Beach. He had just returned after having been away with a sprained foot. He was much distressed about the miserable June 4 battle, and I felt very inclined to say I told you so. I walked up with him to see the L.F.'s, and then back to Aberdeen Gully.

I cannot remember what happened that week, day by day. It was a quiet week and the weather was plea-

sant. We had nights with practically no firing. The
brigade went up into the firing line, I think on Thursday. They had the trenches on the right of the gully.
The L.F.'s stayed down in the support trenches by
the White House, and the R.F.'s and Munsters were
in the firing line, and the Dublins partly in the support
trenches by the gully cemetery. I had one or two services during the week, two in Aberdeen Gully. The
doctors are all very pleasant and nice to be with. They
come out for four days at a time each with their sec-
tions of bearers and orderlies. As a rule they are very
slack with practically nothing to do. I wandered about
during the week a good deal. One day I rode down to
" W " beach to see Hordern, the principal chaplain for
the whole army, who had just arrived from Alexandria
for a couple of nights. He was very nice and we discussed many things. H—— has gone. Other days I
was either down with the regiments on the beach or up
in the trenches or supports to see them. Also Sunday
had to be arranged for. There was very little fighting
on our side all week. The French had a battle, and
made a small advance after a most tremendous bombardment lasting on and off for three days. A most
welcome mail arrived during the week, and I managed
to write a few letters, but seemed to get no opportunity
of writing my diary. Then came Sunday—a busy
day with six services—very hot. I had a service with
the 10th Battery at 11.30, and lunched with them
afterwards. During the afternoon the 368th Battery
across the gully from us was being shelled and the
scrub got on fire. Some men went to put it out,
and one was killed and two wounded. So my service
with them resolved itself into a funeral. Going back
up the gully all was preparation for the coming battle.
I had heard all the details from the artillery people.

I found the L.F.'s bivouacking in the gully and had a little service with them. Then I had one in Aberdeen Gully. I was very tired and went off to bed.

I had an alarming experience that night. I think I have described my little perch cut in the cliff on the right side of the gully. Immediately above it runs a mule-track which goes over to the sea. It is the way by which they carry all provisions to "Y" beach. There was a great deal of bustle that night; mules going to and fro all day. I had the usual internal upset and was lying in my little dug-out. It was covered by a piece of corrugated iron set on some fairly strong posts. I was suddenly awakened about 2 a.m. by the most terrific crash. It seemed as though the whole world was falling on me. I felt I was being buried alive, and struggled into a sitting position, earth pouring off me. I heard a voice shouting and wailing and groaning above me, and I shouted out to ask what on earth they were doing. "Oh, he kicked, sir," was the only answer I could get, followed by more groans. Then a lot of the ambulance people collected. I was sleeping in pyjamas and a dressing-gown, and shouted out I was all right. The whole dug-out was a mass of débris covering all my things. In the middle of it all lay a water tank with the water pouring out. How I was not killed I don't know. It turned out that a mule with two tanks full of water had fallen down about twenty feet onto the top of me, and had then rolled into the gully and trotted off unhurt. I was not even scratched. I slept on a stretcher down below for the rest of the night, and have now made myself a new shelter at the bottom.

The work done by the 87th, 88th, and 89th Territorial

Field Ambulances attached to the 29th Division is deserving of much praise. Being attached to the 89th Field Ambulance, which in turn was attached to the 86th Brigade, I naturally saw most of them. The medical and surgical skill of the doctors was of a very high order, but had little opportunity to show itself. Either there were very few cases coming in, or there was a tremendous rush making it possible to do very little beyond redressing the wounds which had already been dressed at the regimental dressing-stations. But the doctors were very anxious to do what was possible when the rush was not too great to clean up the wounds and perform minor operations, and in many cases managed to do this later on with very beneficial results. They always seemed anxious to do as much work as possible, and were ably supported by the orderlies and stretcher squads. At the 89th we succeeded in making a very snug dressing-station in Aberdeen Gully, where the patients might be secure and undisturbed while shells burst overhead.

Of all the medical work I saw in hospitals and elsewhere, and I saw a great deal, nothing could exceed the devotion of the regimental doctors, orderlies, and stretcher-bearers. The 29th Division was exceptionally fortunate in their medical officers. No matter how fast the cases poured in they went on working till all were attended to. If one regimental dressing-station was full, the nearest doctor would always lend a hand, and on occasions one would find men of various regiments in a regimental dressing-station. The stretcher-bearers went out amidst the greatest danger quite fearlessly to bring in their wounded comrades, and would go on till they dropped with exhaustion. They often had to carry a patient down nearly a mile of narrow trench till they could find the dressing-station, which had to be in a comparatively safe spot, and many lost their lives doing so.

I well remember seeing one of the regimental medical officers one day lying seriously wounded. He had heard that one of the officers in his regiment who had gone out to the attack lay in front of the trench and was still moving. Without hesitation he jumped over the parapet and tried to get to him, but was wounded in the thigh on the way. He had shown singular devotion in his work, and was always ready to assist any regiment when not busy with his own. All the men I saw were enthusiastic about their medical officers.

CHAPTER XI

(June 28—July 14)

Monday, June 28.—Another battle. Oh, how terrible they are ! It began at 10 a.m. in earnest, with a terrific artillery bombardment, which had started the night before. At 11 a.m. the infantry went out and the wounded started to pour in. First the slight cases able to walk, in crowds. Everything seemed to be going well. The Turks were on the run and we had got a line or two of trenches. Then later on in came the stretcher cases, and kept coming all night and next day till about 2 p.m. We had five doctors fortunately, and five wagons working the whole time clearing the wounded down to Gully Beach. In twenty-four hours we had had 500 wounded through, and the 88th, who are next door, about the same number. We were about as full as possible all the time. Eight died here, but were unconscious. The heat was terrific and the flies were simply awful. It was impossible to keep them off. I was not feeling well and was pretty limp. There is little I can do. The men are just longing for the wagons to take them away. We had men from all regiments. The majority seemed to have shrapnel wounds. Our artillery had given such a terrific bombardment that the Turkish infantry simply disappeared and only the guns played on the advancing troops. But the rifle fire started towards evening, when the

146

Dublins lost heavily. I went over to "Y" beach in the afternoon to see how they were getting on there, and found them full of wounded, about 400 cases altogether. An artillery officer was lying there with his leg blown off. He died afterwards. I—— was there, so I did not stop. The L.F.'s and R.F.'s had made the last advance, and I gathered had lost practically all their newly collected officers. I was so tired that I slept part of the night, but was up at dawn. They had been evacuating all night.

Tuesday, June 29.—We had a visit from the General in the morning. He was in a terrible temper. Everything was in a muddle. Where was the medical officer? How many stretchers could he send off at once to J 11, which he had found still full of wounded? Kellas, who was in charge, said he would see. "Don't talk so much. Don't go away. I've got you now. Can you send 6, 50, 500?" "Oh, perhaps six." "Well, send them up immediately under a medical officer." So I volunteered to go as well, and we eventually made a party of seven stretcher squads (four men to a squad), two doctors, and myself. We went up the gully to J 11, the newly captured trench. It was interesting to see the gain of ground and the things left behind by the Turks, especially after having looked at it all so long through a periscope. After many inquiries we found J 11, but understood that there were no wounded, and that the General had been sending all kinds of stretcher squads up. However, we decided we must go, and went a long way along till we got to the Gurkhas. We found one wounded man, and two more were hit while we were there. Meanwhile thirty men had been taken away from their proper employment. The stretcher squads should have been carrying the men from the regimental dressing-station to the Field Ambulance, and we were getting urgent requests for this all the time. However, Generals have to be obeyed, and it was quite interesting. We gained about 1000 yards along the sea-coast and 500 along the gully. The R.F.'s came out with three officers out of the ten and 250 out of the 500 men, the L.F.'s with two officers out of ten and 220 out of 400 men. The Dublins lost ten officers killed and one wounded and 236 men; the Munsters not so heavily. Fitz-Clarence, a fine officer just arrived to the R.F.'s; Floyd, an original Dublin who had been in the *M——* with me; Bousefield, such a nice boy, also an original Dublin, who had been wounded; Taylor, and many others were amongst the killed. The new Lowland Division, just arrived, lost very heavily in the left centre, their Brigadier being killed and three Colonels laid out. The Indian Brigade and the other brigades of the 89th Division also lost a good deal. The total casualties must have been at least 3000 with the usual enormous number of officers. I have since heard that a brigade of the newly arrived Lowland Division, some 3000 strong, went out to take H 12, a trench in front of our left centre. There had been no previous artillery bombardment ! The result—only about 1300 came back, the Brigadier and two Colonels killed and some 1700 men knocked out, practically nothing gained, and almost a whole brigade put out of action. These things seem to happen every battle. The amount of unnecessary lives simply thrown away is appalling. Well, we managed to get pretty clear in the afternoon, though they kept coming in all the time. The 87th Brigade relieved the 86th during the day and the poor remnants of regiments came out for rest. It was a terribly hot day, the hottest we have had, and the water supply to the trenches had been difficult to keep going.

The men looked pretty collapsed when they came out.
The L.F.'s rested in the old support trench. Only
three officers remained : C——, a lieutenant who had
been in France, was in command; Bromley had been
wounded with shrapnel in the heel, but had insisted on
carrying on all night, and then arrived at the dressing-
station; D——, the only other original officer, had
had rather a nasty wound close to the lung. I tried
to fix up a little shelter from the glaring sun for the
three survivors, who were quite played out. Later I
went lower down the gully where the R.F.'s were.
Fortunately their three survivors included C.D.——,
the C.O., and W——, the adjutant. C.D.—— is doing
exceedingly well. He was pretty upset by the battle.
Fitz-Clarence was one of his chief friends. Eustace,
Willet, and Ayreton's bodies had not been recovered.
The difference, as far as I am personally concerned, is
that now I hardly know the officers who are killed.
I did not stay long as they were all so tired. The heat
had finished everybody. I was feeling very well and
fit myself. I carried a man a long way on a stretcher
in the morning.

Major Bromley had come out as adjutant to the 2nd
Lancashire Fusiliers. He had been ship's adjutant on
the A—— on our way out and managed everything
exceedingly well, showing every one unfailing cour-
tesy. This was the second time he had been wounded.
He had been C.O. as well as adjutant for some two or
three weeks previous to the 28th. He had an absolutely cool head and never seemed in the least perturbed or worried, and saw to everything himself. He
was very powerfully built, a splendid gymnast and
swimmer. His wound was not serious, and he recovered from it in Egypt and set sail on the *Royal
Edward*, where he was put in command of all troops
on board some time in August. The *Royal Edward*

was torpedoed on its way to Mudros, and sank. Bromley, so I have since been told, started to swim, but a boat collided with him and stunned him, and he was drowned. In my opinion he was one of the finest soldiers in the Division.

Wednesday, June 30.—The L.F.'s and R.F.'s went down to the beach and stayed there till Saturday night, when they relieved the 88th Brigade. They had a thorough good rest. Another batch of officers arrived, and the R.F.'s now have ten or so and the L.F.'s about six. On Thursday, after lunching with the R.F.'s, I went up to J 12 to try and see if I could discover the bodies of any of the missing officers. I took a guide with me, who said he knew where they had fallen. I went up by Gurkha Bluff and through J 11 A—a long communication trench running along the top of the cliff, parallel with the sea for quite 1000 yards, to J 13 and beyond, which was our main gain. The Turks had retaken J 13 and part of J 12, which were difficult for us to hold, but we have held J 11 A and dug a diagonal trench from the junction of J 11 A and J 13 back to J 11, which is now the firing line. Between J 11 and J 12 the ground was littered with dead. A number of Turks had got cut off and were lying mixed up with our own dead. I went down J 12 and looked through a periscope. A lot of firing was going on and bomb-throwing, so it was impossible to do much, but I was shown where Eustace and Ayreton probably were. The day before I had gone up the gully to look for the bodies of L.F.'s killed on June 4. I took three of the R.A.M.C. with me. They had fallen just in front of J 9. I did want to find Shaw's body. But we found the ground was mostly exposed to fire from across the gully except one small part. There were bodies in all

states of decay, and I saw the worst sights I have yet
seen. However, I can stand most things now. But I
could not touch them. The men did not mind and we
collected a few discs. J 10 had a number of men killed
on the 28th and they were the worst, South Wales
Borderers mostly. It was altogether rather horrible.
I cannot understand why they don't sometimes try and
arrange an armistice and bury the dead. But I have
heard of no attempt having been made. I went down
to the beach again on Friday and Saturday and saw
the regiments. On Saturday I had services with them,
as they were to go up again that night. I also buried
a driver of the 460th Howitzer Battery, and had a very
impressive little funeral with the battery all lined up.
The Major is a most punctilious officer and a splendid
man. I had a good many funerals all through the
week. The greatest care is taken of the graves, and
nice little crosses with names printed on are put up
everywhere. There was a good deal of shelling both
evenings, and I had two rather exciting gallops up the
gully. I think it was Friday evening when word came
that the Turks were massing and bombarding the
trenches on the left, and the regiments on the beach
were to be ready to fall in any moment. They were
shelling the gully, and the batteries on either side. I
sat in a dug-out for some time, but eventually decided
I must go on, and galloped for all I was worth.

Sunday, July 4.—A quiet day. My brigade was all
up in the trenches, so there was nothing much for me
to do. I celebrated at the 88th next door, and then went
a round of batteries : 460th Howitzers, New Zealand,
and 97th R.F.A. While I was at the New Zealand a
huge French transport ship was sunk just off "W"
beach by a submarine and disappeared in about three
minutes. Fortunately she was empty. A French am-

munition dump was also blown up during the afternoon. Rather an unlucky day for them. Then I went
up the gully to the firing line and had a little service
with the Dublin and South Wales Borderers' stretcher-
bearers; then back here for one in Aberdeen Gully for
the ambulances. It is a great opportunity for teaching
just now; men are thinking and experiencing many
things and their thoughts need guiding.

Monday, July 5.—About 3.45 we were awakened by
a most terrific bombardment, which did not really stop
till 10.30. In this little gully it is impossible to know
what is happening. It seemed as though we were
sending the most shells over at first. And then the
Turks sent more and more. They simply flew over in
hundreds. I think we are almost absolutely secure in
here. But shells came as close as possible. Two Jack
Johnsons fell in the 88th gully next door, and one blew
their kitchen to pieces. But they could not get us.
We expected a tremendous influx of wounded but
hardly any one came, perhaps twenty-four altogether,
mostly slight—Dublins. It seemed as though the
bombardment would never end. It rather amused me,
as there was so much noise and so little damage. I
wandered down the gully later on to find out how much
damage had been done, but could hear of very little.
I buried one engineer, and one or two stray men were
killed and wounded. "W" beach had a simply terrific shelling, I believe, and an aeroplane dropped
bombs, but I have not heard of much damage done,
though people were very alarmed there. They are
shelling it continually now and it must be most unpleasant. It appears that the Turks had planned a big
attack, but our guns had got onto them. A good deal
of slaughter was done and the attack broke, and they
did us practically no damage, which is a comfort.

Their shell fire is not particularly accurate, and they simply seemed to drop shells indiscriminately over the peninsula.

Tuesday, July 6.—The South Wales Borderers had a nasty little scrap early this morning over the "Turkey-trot trench," *i.e.* a trench we share with the Turks with a barricade between us. They tried to take a part held by the Turks, and managed to get three officers killed and about ten men; and some twenty-four wounded came in here. I went up and buried some of them. The way officers get killed off is really dreadful, and so unnecessary. I took a funeral service with an R.C. priest. We each said prayers. In the afternoon I went off with T—— (one of the doctors) for a long expedition in the trenches. I wanted to go up and see the brigade. There is a perfect maze of trenches. The brigade is now in the right centre. We got to them through a long winding communication trench used for mules. T—— went back, but I went all the length of the firing line and had tea with the R.F.'s. It was a great joy to find E.F.——back again as adjutant. I got some news from him of wounded officers. He will be a great help to the regiment. C.D.—— makes a splendid C.O. It was quite late before I got back. The men had been having a quiet time in the trenches and were very cheery.

Wednesday, July 7.—I stayed in and wrote most of the morning, made another long trip through the trenches in the afternoon, and found everything again very quiet. A new division of Kitchener's Army has actually arrived and we are really to go off for a little rest. The 87th Brigade goes to-night to Imbros and I expect we go next. I have not seen much of the new divisions. I have lost a good deal of energy and confine it mainly to my own particular job, and cease to take much interest in what goes on outside. It is very hot and the nights are getting warm. I amuse myself by cooking and trying to vary our feeding arrangements, and we now have infinitely superior meals. The soup squares I got from home are specially good. We have porridge every morning for breakfast—a great improvement, and we have actually taught the cook to make toast. I even made some fish cakes one day. We have had masses of chocolate sent out—mostly all melted, though I have been very lucky personally. Parcels were delayed for about a month and we had nothing. Now we have profusion. But biscuits, cake, and tinned fruit are what we like best. However, we cannot complain about food now, though it was getting impossible to eat any more bully this hot weather.

Thursday, July 8.—I rode in to " W " beach in the afternoon. I had not been there for a long time. I wanted to see U—— among other things, but found him out. Of course he had chosen just that day to come out and see me. He hates " W " beach. They are always being shelled there. Our ambulance has been wonderfully lucky. They have not had a man or horse killed yet. I wanted to get some money, but found the field cashier was sick and had gone off, and no one was appointed in his place; so I did not succeed in doing much. When I came back I attempted some baking in a cunningly constructed stove, made out of a zinc ammunition box set into the side of the cliff with a little tin chimney fixed into it. Thompson and Stevens were very amused, because when I started to cook the supper the zinc all melted away and the whole thing collapsed. However, they all acknowledged it was a good idea. I started to read " Paradise Lost " which I am enjoying, and was delighted to find the lines—

> "From morn till noon he fell, from noon till dewy eve,
> On Lemnos, the Ægean Isle."

Friday, July 9.—I kept quiet all day. The mail had arrived the evening before and there were many letters to be written. One must take it quietly now and then in this weather. I had some very delightful letters which cheered me immensely. It is extraordinary how much the mail means to people here and how many letters they write. I think getting and writing letters are the greatest relief from war. One's mind is carried away to other things. People always write apologizing for their petty doings. But these are just what we like. I think we all feel we would like to get away and lead petty uneventful lives for the rest of our existence. I wanted to go round the trenches in the evening and started off, but was blocked by Kitchener's Army, which was swarming up the gully, four deep, a very cheering sight. They seem splendid men, ever so superior to the Territorials we have been getting, much steadier and maturer to look at, and exceedingly keen. They all want to take the hill right away. They have been put into the support trenches, and sent up into the firing line by platoons along with the 29th Division, so as to get gradually accustomed. I decided it was better not to attempt going up that day, so returned.

Saturday, July 10.—I went up to the trenches pretty soon after breakfast and walked through them for miles. First, W——— took me all through the R.F. lines, and carried out a most thorough inspection of the trenches and saw that everything was thoroughly cleaned up. It is really wonderful that the men keep as well as they do. The flies simply swarm everywhere and the place

is strewn with dead bodies. The head of a Turk was
hanging out of the parapet in a sap they were digging ; a heel in another place. It is wonderful how one
gets used to all these sights. The heat would be
really oppressive if it was not that, being on a peninsula, there is usually a breeze blowing from the sea
somewhere. I went all through the 86th Brigade lines
into the Lancs. Territorial lines, and all round through
support trenches, and had no lunch and got very hot
getting back here to tea. I had had another stove
fixed up, made this time of an empty biscuit tin, and
baked some scones. I had no baking-powder, but
they gave me some bicarbonate of soda tabloids, and
with some bacon fat and Ideal milk and sugar and flour
I mixed up my dough and baked some beautiful scones
—more like dough-nuts—their only fault being they
were burnt underneath, which was almost inevitable.
It amused the ambulance men a good deal.

Sunday, July 11.—I had nothing planned, as my
brigade was all up in the firing line. A—— had asked
me to take a service for him on "W" beach. I got
a note at 7.30 a.m. from I—— to say he had gone off
with his brigade to Lemnos, and M——, the newly arrived chaplain, who was to relieve him, had developed
dysentery : would I take a 7 a.m. Celebration ? I called
in on M—— on Gully Beach on my way to "W"
beach and found him very low indeed—almost speech-
less. No service had been held. However, I could
do nothing and walked on to "W" beach. I had some
difficulty in finding the exact spot where the service
was to be. There were about twenty men there, under
a ledge of rock by the lighthouse. Just as we started
they began to fire Black Marias very close to us.
Pieces from the first one dropped exceedingly close
to me. I managed to keep quite calm, but one of

the men, the moment a shell burst, dropped flat on the ground. I think an aeroplane that had just descended was attracting the fire. I went afterwards to the ordnance and succeeded in buying a suit of khaki drill for 8s. 6d. after filling in a number of forms. Then I lunched at the 89th and was given a loan of a horse back to Gully Beach. My horse is temporarily lame and being treated on the beach. He was nearly slain by a Black Maria the night before, which burst very close to him, but he fortunately escaped with a graze. I rode to Gully Beach to see if I could do anything there. I held a little service for the Border Regiment, and tried to arrange one for the Engineers, which did not come off. Then I walked back up the gully, and got in for late tea. I wandered up to the top afterwards to see if anything could be done, but found everything very quiet. Rumours of a battle next day had been prevalent some time. I came back to Aberdeen Gully and had a service at 7 p.m.

Monday, July 12.—They seem to have changed their day for battle from Sunday to Monday. We were warned the night before to be ready. The whole preceding week had been very quiet, practically nothing happening all along the line. We seem to have to wait till we can collect a supply of shells. Well, the main battle was to be on the right. Our end was only subsidiary. The bombardment started at 4.20. The wounded began to come in soon after five. P—— and D—— had come out at midnight to help. It was only a small action at our end—a complete failure. The Dublins were to try to take a Turkish sap. The artillery bombardment failed and the machine guns got onto them, and the majority that went out were knocked out. We had about fifty wounded. P—— worked on the bad cases and gave the deep wounds (there were some horrible ones) a proper cleaning. There were two Dublin officers in but not seriously wounded, and an artillery officer from 368th Battery, also slight. One of the new Kitchener officers was brought in dying, hit through the head. We were kept pretty busy during the early morning, but managed to get them all cleared by about 10 a.m. I had a busy morning. First, I went right up to the firing line to see about burying two Hants men, but their graves were not dug, and I discovered a Kitchener Army chaplain up there who said he would bury them for me. Then I heard that a Dublin stretcher-bearer had been killed and arranged to bury him. The R.F.'s had also had one killed, so I went up through the trenches to P——'s dressing-station and found his body had been carried down to ours. I was afraid the R.F.'s had been in the battle too, and was relieved to find they had not. The battle was on the extreme right, and the French were said to be making good progress. I tried to make it out through the glasses, but it is difficult to see anything. So I returned and buried the Dublin stretcher-bearer (they are all Church of England, being bandsmen), and then came back here and buried the R.F. stretcher-bearer and an artilleryman who had died in the dressing-station.

C—— came in to lunch. It was very hot and he does not like it. It is wonderful how I manage to survive. I am even recovering a good deal of energy. An artillery officer of the 460th Battery arrived to say their sergeant-major had been killed: would I come and bury him? The 460th is a special favourite of mine, and the sergeant-major always used to give the hymn papers round. U—— wanted a meeting of chaplains on "W" beach. The artillery officer lent me his groom's horse and we rode off down the gully

to the beach, where I buried an Australian artillery
captain and arranged for the other funeral, and then
rode on the borrowed horse to Gully Beach, where I
eventually found U—— and A——, and we talked
about many things. U—— thinks services are quite
incongruous with fighting. He says the whole business is so absolutely bloody, and we try and collect
men and sing hymns. We are all a little tired of
hymns. A—— disagreed, thinking the services were
a great relief and meant a lot to the men. Personally
I think they fit in best when the regiments are resting
and away from fighting, as far as it is possible here.
I believe that men are all thinking about things, and
the main thing to do is to try and help them get their
thoughts clear. However, I think we all felt services
were merely incidents. I agree with U——. The
whole thing is indescribably bloody. We have been
here ten weeks and not even seen a civilian, or been
away from shells and the noise of rifle fire. Wounded
and dead everywhere. It almost seems as if it were
normal life now.

A.B.—— and another chaplain appeared later and
we had tea together, with excellent cake, and had a
nice talk. A.B.—— is one of the cheeriest people I
know. He runs about everywhere and holds endless
services, and is always being nearly blown up or
having men disembowelled while taking a service.
But nothing worries him at all. At four o'clock
another battle started, in the centre this time. A
battleship arrived and started to bombard, and there
was a terrific bombardment. But I have lost interest
in battles. I rode back to Gully Beach, and was very
alarmed by a six-inch gun of ours which blazed off a
big shell just over my head as I was passing in front of
it. I met the Major and men of the 460th Battery and we

had a very impressive funeral. The body was carried
up the hill by the sergeants. I halted it as they were
passing through the lines of the battery and took the
first part of the service there. Then we went up to the
grave and finished the service. They started dropping
shells close by. These batteries are very happy families
as a rule. They live close together and see little of any
one else, don't move about, and have comparatively
few casualties. So they feel them all the more when
they do come. I walked back up the gully and made
some beautiful biscuits of dripping, flour, and sugar,
which were really a great success. There seemed to
be a big battle on the right and in the centre going
on intermittently all the time, but we have had no
definite news yet. The poor Lowland Division were
in for it again, but more successful this time I gather.
Personally I have felt it such a relief to have a battle
without the 29th Division being responsible for it. I
cease to take much interest in the military operations.
They are beyond me. And it is useless worrying
about what is going to happen. One can only live
from day to day, and make the best of things as they
come along.

Tuesday, July 13.—I am afraid I spent a large part
of the morning in cooking. I made pastry for the first
time in my life. It really was excellent. I made a
large jam tart, using just flour, dripping, and sugar and
spreading apricot jam on it. It took about two hours
to do, as I had to keep a very slow fire to prevent it
burning—but I must say it was a wonderful success.
We were expecting company, which, however, did not
come. In the afternoon I went off with A—— and
visited one or two of the batteries, seeing young L——
at No. 10. They had constructed a most beautiful
dug-out and made themselves exceedingly comfortable

all roofed with tin, the sides cut into the solid rock,
and were even covered with mosquito netting, so quite
free from flies. We sat and ate Fuller's sweets.
At No. 97 there is a little spring where we got some
beautiful maidenhair plants, which we took back and
decorated the mess with. I buried four men of the
mountain battery that night. They had all been killed
at their gun. It was strange knowing that pretty terrific fighting was going on somewhere all the time, and
being so out of it and knowing nothing of what was
going on. Our wing, for a change, was quiet.

Wednesday, July 14.—I started off on a visit to the
trenches in the afternoon, but only to hear on the way
that the brigade was at last coming out of the trenches
after eleven solid days. I went to brigade headquarters to see if I could find out what they were
going to do and when they were going away. But
they had heard nothing. So I came back again, finding the R.F.'s headquarters staff getting things ready
for the night in a bivouac at the head of the gully.
I arranged to return to supper. They were jolly glad
to get out, but had had very few casualties fortunately,
and no attacks to make.

M

CHAPTER XII

MUDROS AGAIN

(*July* 15—*August* 9)

Thursday, July 15.—I first met W—— at 9 a.m. at the R.F.'s, and we went off to hunt for Shafto's grave. They had just had orders to move down to the beach. So when the regiment had started, we set off through the usual labyrinth of trenches, into the mule-track, and then along it till we saw a ruined house with a large fig-tree beside it, underneath which his grave was. It had a nice cross, and was elaborately decorated with shell cases. I said a few prayers. We hunted for Anstice's grave as well, but could not find it. Then we rejoined the regiment on the beach. I had a little lunch with G. H——, and amused myself watching the men lining up and being dealt out a complete new set of clothing. Orders arrived that the regiment was to be prepared to move any moment. So I returned to Aberdeen Gully, and got my servant to pack up all my things. A cart had fortunately just come out, which took them down. I rode back, going round for the first time along the road which has been constructed the whole way from Gully Beach to " W " beach at the foot of the cliff, and so under cover. At " W " beach I repacked everything, and after supper went down to " V " beach, where the brigade was assembling ready to go off. It was quite dark. All " V " beach is open in the middle, and the troops were just lying down waiting till mine-sweepers

NULLAH ON SIDE OF BIG GULLY, WITH ROYAL FUSILIERS' RATION DUMP

should come and take them off. We were told the
first would be there at 11 p.m. However, nothing
happened, and we were soon off to sleep. Suddenly,
at midnight, Asiatic Annie started, and dropped a
Black Maria very close to us. Everybody jumped
up. I know I rushed for a dug-out I had previously
spotted. A number of men literally dived in on top
of me. I think we were all so confused with sleep
we did not know what was happening. Then all the
men were drawn up under the shelter of a stack of
supply boxes, and we all remained pretty calm while,
fortunately, the remaining shells travelled farther and
farther over our heads. But it was singularly alarming at the moment. This sort of thing happens
every night on the beaches. Then we had another
long wait. Eventually a trawler appeared at about
2.30. Kitchener's Army was being landed as we were
being taken off. About 250 of us crowded on board,
and we were taken off to a mine-sweeper, which the
skipper had great difficulty in finding in the dark.
At last we found her. She had to put troops off
onto our boat while we got on her. Eventually we
got on board. Most of us discovered some spot
where we managed to get a little sleep. I found a
large armchair in a little saloon. We awoke to find
ourselves still anchored off "W" beach, with a lot of
goods on board which had to be shipped off onto a
lighter. This took a long time. While it was going
on, shells suddenly started again. This time they
were aimed at a supply boat close to us. She got up
steam and made off as quickly as possible, and we did
the same, taking the lighter with us, and loading her
all the time. Then when that was done we had to go
alongside the hospital ship and take some cases on
board, and at last we started off for Lemnos, getting

there about 4 o'clock. It was very pleasant and peaceful on board. At Lemnos there was another long wait till boats came and took us off. We landed at dusk, and marched off to our camping-ground, which we found in the middle of a field where vegetable marrows, maize, and other vegetables were growing. Some of the regiment had arrived before us. G—— had returned, and taken over command. I had decided to join a company mess, and found G. H——, with a couple of attached Australian officers, under a fig-tree. They said I was to be mess president. These Kitchener officers are so different to the regulars. G. H—— coached the Cambridge Eight last year to victory. He is a splendid fellow. There was another fellow there who seemed to consider himself a bit of a poet, and appeared to know a good deal about literature. Another captain is a dentist. But the variety makes conversation far more interesting. The Australians seemed nice. One was Australian born, the other had only recently gone out. We were soon asleep under the fig-tree, and spent a very peaceful night, away at last from the sound of firing and shells.

Saturday, July 17.—The officers of Y Company made me their mess president. We were only five in all, but decided to celebrate our holiday by as good a mess as possible. So, escorted by two orderlies, I spent the morning in the village buying pots and pans of every description, and quantities of fresh vegetables, marrows, French beans, egg fruit, tomatoes, melons, little pears, nuts, as well as tinned butter, fruit, rice, lemons, eggs, and other delicacies. It is quite easy to make a table. You simply dig a square trench. The centre of the square is the table, and you sit round it, with your feet in the trench.

We got a pretty good cook, and I showed him how to make omelettes, macaroni cheese, milk puddings, and other things. We even managed to get fresh milk and native wine, and bought large earthenware jars, one of which was kept full of lemonade. Fresh meat was provided as a ration, so we did very well, and had a very happy party. In the afternoon I arranged my services, walked to the top of a neighbouring hill with G. H—— to get the view, and came back to hold an extempore sing-song for the brigade in a large tent that happened to be empty. It was not a great success. I could not get the men to sing. I've heard the other brigades held much better ones. But it was got up in too great a hurry.

Sunday, July 18.—I held my parades in front of the same tent at 7 and 9.30. I had Ante-Communion in each case, followed by Celebrations, but very few stayed, only six at the first, and twelve at the latter. I was rather surprised. In the afternoon I walked over to a neighbouring village, and we got some wine. It was full of soldiers, mostly Dublins, having a good drink. The authorities seemed to have made no restrictions, though they did afterwards. I also had to go to Mudros to get more provisions. I am afraid we do not observe Sunday much. I had a little voluntary evening service later on.

Monday, July 19.—A new Captain for Y Company (I cannot remember his name) had arrived with a draft. He had a friend in the ordnance, and had been off to see him, and got an order on one of the ships for a mess tent. So off I went with him in the afternoon to get it. We chartered a native sailing-boat, and eventually got to our ship, and went aboard. I found a lot of ambulance men who had come with a new division. I had tea with the doctors, who introduced me to the purser, from whom I got a sack of oatmeal—all he could spare me, but a great luxury. The Captain changed his order for one tent to two tents, with permission of the ordnance officers, and we returned with a boat loaded with two large E.P. tents (*i. e.* double tents, as used in India). We managed to get hold of a motor-lorry after a good deal of trouble, and got the tents up to the camp, where one was presented to headquarters. They are wonderfully cool tents, but very bulky and cumbersome. When we had ours put up it was without its curtains, so the Captain had to return next day for them. We felt well satisfied, and set up for a nice comfortable rest. However, it was not to last long.

Tuesday, July 20.—I awoke with a temperature and throat. I did not seem to improve, and at midday found my temperature nearly 102, so sent for the doctor, who said I had an influenza cold, and must go to hospital. A large new draft of 200 men, and more officers, arrived that morning. But the poor brigade were suddenly ordered to return the next day. So all our preparations had been in vain. It turned out a false alarm. They were fearing a big Turkish attack which never came off, and they had nothing to do. Meanwhile, I wandered off with my servant and kit in search of a hospital, of which there seem to be many. The first I came to said they were very sorry, but they were not for my division; I must go to the 16th Stationary Hospital. So we started off again. It was very hot. At last I found the orderly-room, where an orderly said they were full up. I got a little exasperated then, and said, "Am I to wander round the island, with a temperature of 102, looking for a hospital?" However, a doctor soon arrived, and said it was quite all right; of course I could come in.

They were very full. Would I mind a bell tent? I
said, "Of course not." So I was put on a stretcher in
a bell tent, and slept the whole time. They did not
pay much attention to me. The doctor neither took
my temperature nor looked at my throat, but sounded
me very carefully, though I assured him heart and
lungs were quite all right. Next day he transferred
me to a proper marquee, a double tent, where I was
put in a bed with sheets made of the same canvas as
the tent, but with a large mosquito net over it to keep
off the flies. W—— was in the corner of it, recovering from dysentery.

Wednesday, July 21.—I spent a peaceful day, but
my throat got worse. Still the doctor did not look
at it. Next day (*July* 22) I again complained of
my throat. In fact, I could hardly speak, so he
examined it, and looked very grave. He said I
might be infectious, and asked me to get inside the
mosquito netting. Eventually he returned with
another doctor, who also examined my throat. I
asked if he would disclose the nature of my disease.
At first he refused, but returned later to say I should
have to be moved to a bell tent by myself, and that
he was afraid I had diphtheria. I was not in the
least alarmed, as I did not feel particularly ill, only
I had a very uncomfortable throat, and I was carried
off to a bell tent. Here I found a stretcher put ready
for me on a couple of boxes. At this I did complain.
I said I was supposed to have a serious complaint, and
was to be kept in hospital some weeks. Was I to lie
on a stretcher all the time, while men with mild attacks
of dysentery, who were able to be up and about all
day, were given beds to sleep on? So a bed was soon
forthcoming, and I must say ever since they have
done everything to make me comfortable. An excel-

lent orderly, a trained male nurse, waited on me; and my servant, who had been entered into the hospital with something the matter with his foot, came in and lived in the tent with me, and has waited on me hand and foot ever since, disinfecting himself with carbolic and gargle under strict directions from the doctor. That evening the doctor gave me an injection of serum. It gave almost instantaneous relief. The next day (*Friday, July* 23) he gave me two more injections. Of course, I ate practically nothing all the time, and did nothing except talk to an occasional visitor. A—— was very good about coming in. His brigade (the 88th) stayed several days after mine left. By Sunday, July 25, I felt much better. D——, the chaplain on the island, brought me Communion in the morning, and I started to read, and have read a good deal ever since. They tried to get me off on a ship at first, but they refused to have me. People seem to be very afraid of diphtheria. The doctor is alarmed of after effects, and has allowed me to do nothing. It is now (*August* 4) over a fortnight since I came in. The weather has not been too hot as a rule, though we have had one or two bad days. To-day has been one. My servant lifts the skirt of the tent up all round, and pins a blanket on the outside between me and the sun. If it is very hot I lie on a stretcher on the ground, and catch any possible draught. I have canvas sheets, but they are better than none. I have also got a deck-chair, in which I am now sitting. The 89th Field Ambulance were here until recently, and occasionally some of the doctors came to see me. I got my mail while they were here, which was nice. A parcel mail brought me some welcome biscuits, cheese, toffee, and a nice supply of stationery. We actually have a man who comes round and sells *The Times*, only about ten days old, at fourpence a copy. Otherwise we hear nothing of the outer world. My tent looks out over the harbour, so I can amuse myself watching the troops coming and going. Nothing seems to have happened while I have been here, but now reports are coming in of a new landing having been made, and there has been a large exodus of troops yesterday and to-day. I do hope they are not attacking to-day, as it is so hot, and our men cannot stand the heat. It is the anniversary of the declaration of war. The hospitals have been told to be as empty as possible by to-morrow. This one is fuller than ever. It is only supposed to take in 200 cases, and has about 800, mostly slight. It came out with the 29th Division, and has worked without stopping since the beginning. The orderlies are quite worn out, and keep going sick. Mine went sick some days ago. They toil on with temperature up to 103 before they drop. They are very short-handed. All the other hospitals are moving to the other side of the harbour. They have till now all been crowded together close to the village, on ground formerly occupied by the French horse lines, now one mass of dust and sand, which the wind blows about in clouds. No wonder the orderlies go sick. However, the authorities have at last woken up to the extent of realizing that the other side of the harbour, away from dust, villages, and horse lines, is likely to be more sanitary. Meanwhile, we stay here, and take in everybody's patients.

My servant has taken admirable care of me. I am not allowed meat yet, and hospital fare unsupplemented would be bad. However, he makes me beautiful toast, poaches eggs, and fries me tomatoes. Otherwise I get porridge, soup, potatoes, and milk pudding. I am getting quite hungry now. The doctor says I may take a little walk to-morrow. I hope to get away next week on a ship, perhaps to Alexandria. I may not work or exert myself this month. They are so afraid of after effects. I expostulate, saying people must take chances in war-time. But the doctor says I take quite enough chances by having the disease at all. I really feel perfectly well, and almost strong again. I am very fortunate to have got off so lightly. The doctor takes the greatest care of me. He is young, but served in the Bulgarian Red Cross in the Balkan War. He hates the Bulgars, and would not own them as Allies. I think he is rather pleased at having got me well so soon. A new sergeant-major for the hospital has just arrived. I heard him saying that he was only released from prison in Germany three weeks ago, and then sent straight here. What a strange war! Well, this is all about myself—but what else have I to write about?

There is nothing much more to record about my time in No. 16 Stationary Hospital, Lemnos. On Thursday, August 5, I was allowed out in the evening for the first time. The next day the pathologist, who by now had arrived, declared that I was free from infection. I started to have my meals with the other invalid officers in the mess tent. They were mostly mild dysentery cases from Kitchener's Army, two from Oxford, and it was nice having some talk. I wandered round the village once or twice. Of course I was pretty shaky, but, as usual, recovered very rapidly. My name was put down for a hospital ship. The doctor would not hear of my returning to the peninsula. Meanwhile rumours were growing fast. A huge battle to last five days was about to begin. The hospital was to be prepared for enormous casualties.

Sunday, August 8.—I was able to go to church three times. Then the first casualties arrived, mainly from the old battle front. A huge attack had started on Friday, again on H 12, where so many lives had already been lost. The 88th Brigade, filled with large drafts, had gone out, and the Worcesters especially had lost enormously. I do not think the 86th lost as much. Nothing seems to have been gained. C——, one of the R.F.'s, arrived with dysentery, and gave some account of what had happened. Major F—— had been knocked over by a shell. I have seen no R.F.'s since, so hope all is well with them. Meanwhile, the main fighting had been up at Anzac, and beyond, where a new landing had been made. Three new divisions had been landed altogether, and I have since seen a lot of their wounded. But what the net result has been it is impossible to say. They seem to have got a good way inland. Of course the casualties have been simply colossal; no one knows how many. Every available hospital ship was crammed. Some said the operations were intended to be of a decisive nature, regardless of cost. But I do not believe decisive operations are possible in this war. At any rate, it seems impossible to know anything, or to get any really trustworthy information.

Monday, August 9.—I had given up much hope of going onto a hospital ship, owing to all the fighting, when in the afternoon I suddenly got word to be ready to go off in a quarter of an hour. Of course we did not go till some three hours later. We got onto a hospital ship, the *Sicilia*, one of the original ones. Needless to say, we were in clover. I felt such a fraud. But the doctor insisted I must go. I slept with other mild cases in hammocks on the deck ; much the coolest place, and quite comfortable. The food was extraordinarily good, quite plain, but very well cooked, and I was ravenous. Most of the day I slept and read. There was a nice matron on board, and a number of stalwart nurses, who were pretty well overworked. One told me she had 114 patients, each of whom she had to dress or look after. There were a good many bad cases on board, and the Chaplain showed me a list of forty funerals in five days. I had an exceedingly pleasant and comfortable voyage, and felt ever so much better for it, reaching Alexandria on Thursday, 12th August.

POSTSCRIPT

HERE my connection with the 29th Division ended, just as the new landing at Suvla Bay was made, and the campaign started on its second and final despairing phase. I am in no position to say anything about it at first hand. I returned to Mudros on September 1, remaining there till the end of the year, organizing a scheme of recreations and canteens for the troops in hospitals, rest and reinforcement camps. But though I often came across members of the 29th Division, I had no further official connection with it. The last news I have is that of the Royal Fusiliers' officers, who were present at the first landing, only one, who had been wounded, and the quartermaster, were left with the battalion. One single R.F. alone had come through the whole campaign from the landing to the evacuation. But long before the time I left it the 29th Division, though continuing the same in name, was unrecognizable as the magnificent unit I had come out with. There was much more work for it to do, and it continued to bear the brunt of the fighting after the Suvla Bay landing right up to the evacuation of the peninsula. There are many other divisions both in France, in the Dardanelles and elsewhere, which have covered themselves with imperishable glory, but it may be doubted whether any have played a more striking, picturesque, and inconceivably difficult part than the 29th and the Australian and New Zealand contingents. From the beginning of opera-

173

tions till the final close they continued on the peninsula, with practically no rest and change. They were continually in the forefront of the battle. Their casualties were appalling, and their ranks were thinned by sickness and frost-bite. The regiments had continually to be made up with large drafts from England, and their officers were constantly changing. But these new and only partially trained men seemed to catch some of the inspiration of those who preceded them.

It has been impossible, where numbers were so great, to make special reference to any of the N.C.O.'s and men, and only a few officers have been referred to by name with whom I was especially brought into contact. But the acts of heroism and perseverance might be multiplied indefinitely, and those mentioned must serve merely as samples of the rest.

In the eyes of the world the whole expedition appears to have been a complete failure. But those who saw anything of the valour and endurance of the officers and men who took part in it cannot accept this verdict. They conquered where others would have failed; and whoever may be blamed by future historians for our failure to get through to Constantinople, it will not be the men who did the fighting. They showed themselves worthy of the greatest military traditions, and, in the words of Brigadier-General Hare, "the men of Albuhera and Minden, of Delhi and Lucknow, will be proud to hail them, as their equals in valour and military achievement."

ADDITIONAL CHAPTER

(The following vivid account has been contributed by Major H. M. Farmar, D.S.O., of the Lancashire Fusiliers, Staff-Captain and then Brigade-Major to the 86th Brigade.)

THE LANDING OF THE 86TH INFANTRY BRIGADE UNDER BRIGADIER-GENERAL S. W. HARE, ON THE GALLIPOLI PENINSULA, 25TH APRIL 1915, AND ITS SUBSEQUENT OPERATIONS

ON the 23rd April 1915, ship after ship steamed out of Mudros Harbour—each packed with soldiers, English, Scotch, Irish, New Zealanders, Australians, French troops, black Senegalese, part of the Foreign Legion—through the line of battleships and smaller war-craft, both British and French. The Australians led the way and made the air ring with resounding cheers; these were replied to by the sailors, and taken up by each transport in turn with inspiring enthusiasm. The Lancashire Fusiliers were divided between H.M.S. *Euryalus* and H.M.S. *Implacable;* the Royal Fusiliers in H.M.S. *Implacable;* the Royal Munster and the Royal Dublin Fusiliers in the S.S. *River Clyde;* the Brigade Headquarters in the mine-sweeper S.S. *Whitby Abbey.* The exchange from the transports was made after the arrival at Tenedos.

On the 25th April the brigade paraded to the sound of the bombardment, a thunder of ships' guns about the coast in the first light of dawn, and made ready to disembark.

As the *Whitby Abbey* stood in towards the beach east of Cape Helles, aimed fire began to strike the ship, and men were killed and wounded as they stood paraded on the deck ready to file into the boats. There was no cover. The men-o'-war boats came alongside, arranged in tows of four or five, to be taken close in by steam pinnaces. They made one trip from the *Euryalus,* and had to be cleared of dead and wounded before others could file into them from the *Whitby Abbey.* When the steamboat could get no closer the bluejackets took to their oars, the boats were separated and made for the beach.

There was no confusion, but it was not easy to be quick, as the boats were crowded and some of the rowers were hit. Little re-adjustments had to be made to let soldiers get to vacant oars. The Brigade Staff landed with the Lancashire Fusiliers on beach "W." The Brigadier and Major Frankland, Brigade-Major, had seen the first party of Lancashire Fusiliers, who were put ashore in the middle of the beach, suffer severely in the barbed wire entanglements near the water's edge and up the sandy slope. They were subjected to a cross fire of machine guns and rifle fire.

The Brigadier and Major Frankland stood up and diverted all the boats they could to the left, where the men were able to land under a certain amount of cover afforded by the cliffs. The survivors on the beach forced their way through and past the wire and pushed forward up the centre of the little valley leading from the shore, Captain Willis, Captain Tallents, and Lieutenant Seckham displaying the utmost gallantry.

Major Adams' company had made for the cliff edge on the left of the beach, which they took, and ensconced themselves in some Turkish trenches. The Brigadier with Major Frankland, followed by a few men, went up the cliff still further to the left. The men, handicapped by their heavy packs and burden of ammunition, had difficulty in getting up the very steep bits near the top, and the officers found themselves on the plateau with half-a-dozen men and the Turks only twenty to forty yards distant. These were firing at Major Adams' company.

Major Frankland took a rifle from a man and shot three Turks, if not a fourth. More men arrived and went for the enemy, who gave way. The Brigadier and Brigade-Major then reconnoitred towards the direction in which the Royal Fusiliers were expected to appear, and on their return the Brigadier was severely wounded. Seeing that all was going well on the left, Major Frankland visited the company next on the right to get them to conform and go forward.

The adjutant, Captain Bromley, who was at this point, set the men an example of fearlessness which they cheerfully followed. There is no doubt that the action of the Brigadier in landing with the foremost in this unprecedented enterprise, together with Frankland's mastery of the situation after the General was wounded, were together largely responsible for success.

Each separate party to land found itself with an individual task to perform and was at once closely engaged. At a moment when the troops were enduring the effects of a bewildering shock they were given a course to pursue with confidence and cohesion.

The Lancashire Fusiliers had the task on which depended the success of the troops landing on the beaches right and left of them. Had they failed the others must have been destroyed. A message came

N

through from the Royal Fusiliers that they had landed north of Cape Helles without much opposition. The attention of the Turks had been arrested by the Lancashire Fusiliers. It was arranged for the two battalions to fight for a junction and to secure themselves pending a further advance.

No news had come in from the remaining two battalions of the brigade, who were to land from the ex-collier *River Clyde* in the little haven of Sedd-el-Bahr on the right; and no troops appeared to have moved on to the high ground on that side of beach "W."

The Brigade-Major and Staff-Captain, returned to the beach with the idea of getting troops forward on to Hill 138 and Hill 141, to take the Turkish redoubts thereon, and to assist the advance of the Royal Munster and Royal Dublin Fusiliers from Sedd-el-Bahr, also to establish Brigade Headquarters at the ruined lighthouse, which had previously been named as a spot to which all reports should be sent when a footing had been secured. This lighthouse proved to be within two hundred yards of a Turkish redoubt, but was close to the edge of the cliff.

Captain Haworth was reorganizing the remnant of his company, the first to land, on the beach : only about fifty were left of the double company, and there were also there twelve men of Captain Shaw's company under Second Lieutenant Beaumont. The first effort to reach the high ground here by Captain Haworth had been foiled by a heavy explosion on the cliff edge just as it was reached. The men had literally been blown back, and there had been many casualties. Porter was killed here.

Amongst and beyond a long barbed wire entanglement, which had been enfiladed by machine guns, were the still forms of many score. Such a charge

from the water's edge must these men have made.
The dead dotted behind them upon the sand bore
witness to the fire through which they had run. Captain Maunsell, Captain Thomas and Lieutenant Wil-
liamson were there in the foremost lines, fallen with
the comrades of many years in work and sport:
comradeship that keeps lit the spirit of the regiment,
and on this day made possible the sacrifice and the
success.

Major Frankland explained what was required, and
led, under cover of the cliff, to the lighthouse. It was
then found that Captain Shaw had moved his company
on to the high ground immediately on the right of
beach "W," and his initiative had undoubtedly secured us from an immediate counter attack on this
flank, and also assisted very materially to further Major
Frankland's plan. Captain Haworth extended his men
below the crest of the cliff, along a ledge, and then
moved them towards a redoubt which could be seen
close behind an exceedingly thick entanglement of
barbed wire. Second Lieutenant Beaumont was sent
with his twelve men to the ridge which connected the
high ground of Hill 138 with that of Hill 141, dominat-
ing Sedd-el-Bahr. Both parties got as far as the wire
and then could get no further: there was a fold of
ground in which the men could lie without much risk,
and the Turks could not fire directly into it without
exposing themselves. Any effort to cut the wire
proved to be courting instant death.

Lieutenant Cunliffe came up with a small party of
machine gunners but without machine guns. He took
up a position between Captain Shaw and Captain
Haworth. In landing Lieutenant Cunliffe had been
launched into deep water and swam ashore, wearing his
full equipment with heavy pack and rifle. It was a

feat which only a very fine swimmer could have performed, and it was under fire. Later, he collected his gun teams and took them to fill the gap described, thereby linking up the battalion, which henceforward had perfect internal communication and occupied a position which fulfilled all that was required of it— a result attained by the skill and boldness of Captain Willis and Captain Shaw, the perspicuity of Cunliffe, and by the tenacity of Captain Haworth.

Near the lighthouse the ground rose gently to the right and up to a ridge which commanded both the ground we occupied and also, on the far side, the ground above Sedd-el-Bahr. Captain Haworth was liable to enfilade from here, and an occupation by the Turks of this ridge would have been very dangerous.

Second Lieutenant Beaumont with his twelve men was placed to protect this flank. It is a mystery why no counter-attack was made; there were a considerable number of Turks in the two redoubts and in the fort above Sedd-el-Bahr, and these kept up a brisk fire.

At about 8.30 a.m. Major Frankland made a personal reconnaissance to endeavour to find a way of assisting the troops landing from the *River Clyde*. He stood up to use his glasses and was killed instantly. The Staff-Captain then temporarily assumed command of the brigade. He established his headquarters under cover of the ruins of the lighthouse, which gave a shelter of a space of about eight yards by four.

The Signal Section got into touch with Divisional Headquarters on board H.M.S. *Euryalus,* with the *River Clyde* aground at Sedd-el-Bahr, and with the Royal Fusiliers. This section consisted of Royal Engineers, Territorial Force. Their efficiency and coolness were remarkable, and it was their first experience under fire. Captain King and Sergeant Spears

set an example which was lived up to by every one of
the section, and maintained throughout all the following most arduous operations. All the day the Turks
sniped Brigade Headquarters and Captain Haworth's
men : it was difficult to locate whence the fire came.
About a dozen men were hit.

About 11 a.m. Captain Haworth was shot through
the back and body, but he refused to be moved, and
continued to command his men until four o'clock in
the afternoon, when reinforcements of two battalions
came up and took the redoubts.

The Royal Fusiliers sent in precise and accurate
reports : they got into communication with the 87th
Brigade on their left, and complied with the order to
co-operate with the Lancashire Fusiliers in pushing
back the enemy sufficiently far to give freedom in
landing more troops on beach " W."

The Worcestershire and Essex battalions of the 88th
Brigade began operations about 2 p.m., and by 5.20
p.m. they had the Turkish positions on Hill 138 in
their hands. The troops then entrenched themselves.

Divisional Headquarters remained on board H.M.S.
Euryalus, where touch with all landings was obtained
by wireless, but Colonel Wolley-Dod, General Staff,
landed at beach " W " during the afternoon to control
operations in the vicinity, and at 7 p.m. sent for the
Staff-Captain to assist him.

Throughout this day at Brigade Headquarters there
was doubt as to the exact situation at Sedd-el-Bahr.
By running from the lighthouse and then slipping
over the edge of the cliff, a position could be reached
from which the *River Clyde* could be seen ; and visual
communication was established with the 88th Brigade
Signal Section, who worked behind iron plates on the
bridge of the collier.

By gingerly picking a way it was possible to reach a point above some men who had landed from the ex-collier and to shout to them. They could get no further, and the cliff was unclimbable. There were very few and almost all wounded. There appeared to be a line of men holding a ridge across the beach, but who made no progress. It transpired later that they were dead, cut down by machine-gun fire as they made a rush. The messages, which came by helio, gave the impression that great difficulties were being encountered. In fact, on that day "V" beach was impossible to live upon, and, almost, to land upon, although attempt after attempt was made. The Commanding Officer was killed : the troops left on board were sheltering behind iron plating.

The night of the 25th April was dark. The 1st/5th Battalion Royal Scots (Territorials) were landed on beach "W" as a reserve, and some working parties of the Royal Naval Division. The survivors of the troops in the *River Clyde* landed at Sedd-el-Bahr and began their task ashore. The Turks attacked the position covering beach "W." The reserve had to be used, and then every man with a rifle, servants, police, orderlies. It began to rain and was cold.

The Signal Section had to vacate their position, and communication was cut off except by means of orderlies, who had to work over strange ground, and these only brought in requests for reinforcements, of which there were none. The volume of fire was very great. Captain Willis did great service during this night in establishing a feeling of cool confidence in his portion of the line, and this spread; no ground was lost that had been so hardly won.

On the 26th April the troops from Sedd-el-Bahr cleared the village, captured the old Castle Ridge, and,

in conjunction with the troops on Hill 138, cleared
Hill 141. The Royal Munster Fusiliers and Royal
Dublin Fusiliers with a half-battalion of the Hampshire regiment, organized by Colonel Doughty Wylie,
and led by him and such officers as Majors Grimshaw
and Molesworth, Tomlinson, Nightingale, and Walde-
grave, did magnificently. Their force of arms drove
back superior numbers of the Turks from their points
of vantage and into headlong rout. The fallen Grimshaw was spoken of as might have been Roland of
Charlemagne's day by the witnesses of his deeds in
the throes of close combat.

The position won was quickly secured and consoli-
dated under the direction of Colonel Williams, an
officer of Sir Ian Hamilton's Staff, and the Brigade-
Major of the 86th Brigade, Major Molesworth and a
few remaining officers doing the work of a score in
reorganizing. The men, though deprived of most of
their accustomed leaders, worked quietly according to
their thorough training.

Colonel D. E. Cayley of the Worcestershire regiment was appointed temporarily to command the
brigade, and Captain Kane, Royal Munster Fusiliers,
assumed the duties of Staff-Captain, the latter having
been promoted to be Brigade-Major.

On the 28th April the 86th Brigade, having reorgan-
ized, was at first employed in reserve. At 8 a.m. they
entrenched a position in support of the main attack,
which was being pressed forward by the French on
the right, the 88th Brigade in the centre, and 87th
Brigade on the left. Only general instructions could
be given for the movement, as the situation ahead could
not be gauged, and it was necessary to take risks to
reap advantage from the success already gained. It
was possible that the Turks might not stand before the

position of Achi Baba was captured. Delay meant that the Turks would gain heart, and also more guns and reinforcements. It was a big risk, to advance without reconnaissance and without artillery support, the thin line of infantry stretching across the peninsula, and no weight anywhere with which to carry through an assault. The guns of the ships could not give the close support necessary for infantry owing to the flatness of their trajectory. But it was necessary. Ground had to be gained to give safety in disembarking stores, men, and guns, and to support other landings. The attempt, in spite of slender numbers, achieved much success.

At 11.30 a.m. Major-General Marshall, who was temporarily commanding the three brigades of British infantry, gave orders for the 86th Brigade to join in the main attack. The 88th Brigade were in difficulties and were short of ammunition. The 86th Brigade received orders to take forward ammunition for the 88th, and to carry the latter on in the advance to the objective given. This was a spur lying north-east of Krithia, and involved the capture of this village. The Royal Fusiliers and the Lancashire Fusiliers were given written orders; and the firing line and supports for the attack were organized in a nullah, under cover, and launched under the command of Major Bishop. The Royal Munster Fusiliers and the Royal Dublin Fusiliers formed the reserve. Major Pearson was given the task of organizing the ammunition supply.

The written orders, issued to the four battalions, named a point of direction for the first phase of the advance, a prominent white mosque at the western end of Krithia village. The left platoon of the Lancashire Fusiliers, under Second Lieutenant Needham, was given the duty of directing the advance; the Royal

Fusiliers were on the left. The whole line was given orders to conform to the movements of the directing platoon. Commanding officers were interviewed personally by the Brigadier, who explained the situation and the orders. Then the advance began.

At this juncture the French, on the right, appeared to be retiring from the ground they had taken earlier in the day. The 88th Brigade were in difficulties, and a Staff Officer sent back for assistance. Unluckily the message did not reach Headquarters, but did reach some portions of both the Royal Munster Fusiliers and the Royal Dublin Fusiliers, and some of these were diverted, unorganized, into the 88th Brigade, and lost touch with their own.

These battalions had lost many officers on the 25th and 26th, and were moving in small parties, in artillery formation, to avoid the effect of shrapnel fire. In consequence the 86th Brigade lost the power of giving weight to their movement. It was a most unfortunate accident. The Brigade-Major was sent to collect as many as he could get touch with, and returned with those he found to Brigade Headquarters.

Major Pearson had now got up some ammunition on pack animals. Reports were received that the 87th Brigade on the left was held up by entrenchments. Major-General Marshall gave orders for the ammunition to be taken forward and for the 86th Brigade to push on. Some fifty of the Royal Dublin Fusiliers loaded themselves with bandoliers full of ammunition, and were led to the firing line by the Brigade-Major. The firing line was found to be taking advantage of some natural cover, and was sufficiently protected to avoid many casualties. It was packed and stationary.

The ammunition party, by good fortune, had come up near to Second Lieutenant Needham with the directing platoon. The ammunition was passed down the line and the party sent back under Sergeant Fergusson, R.D.F., whose services were most valuable. Orders brooked no delay, and there was no change of plan. Training has been to mutually support advance and to conform to movement.

Captain Shaw was next to Second Lieutenant Needham, and arranged to cover his advance with fire. Word was passed down the line that an advance was about to take place. Then Needham, with about fifty men, made a rush.

The adjutant, Captain Bromley, dashed out with them. Some of the Royal Fusiliers under Cripps and O'Connell conformed and moved forward on the left. The Turks fired very accurately, and the rushes had to be short and quick. The movement was exhilarating and rapid. A certain number of men were lost, but by one bit of the line covering the other with short bursts of rapid fire, a wood was reached, afterwards known as the Twelve Tree Wood. This was very shallow and had thick undergrowth. Here were found many dead and wounded Turks.

Captain Bromley and Second Lieutenant Needham and the Brigade-Major, with Sergeant Burtchael and a few men, went through the wood, down a heathery slope into a shallow depression, and up into some cover on the opposite rise leading to Krithia.

The buildings on the outskirts could be clearly seen, and Turks running back and jumping into some small quarries. Shouts for the line to come forward met with no response. Probably the men who had made the rapid advance were exhausted, carrying heavy packs and 200 rounds of ammunition. Officers had been wounded, and it is probable that no one responsible was left unwounded who knew that the little party had gone beyond the wood to reconnoitre while reorganization was taking place. Seckham had been wounded in the wood. Captain Bromley offered to go back and bring on the line : he made a movement to go and was shot through the knee. Sergeant Burt-chael took him back, and they joined Captain Willis, who had brought his men up near the wood, and Captain Shaw was close by on his left.

The little party remained in observation and were able to make a good reconnaissance, then, as no further advance was made, the Turks began to come back. A private soldier of the Royal Dublin Fusiliers was hit in the groin, and when he was bound up, those remaining crawled back with him into the undergrowth of the slope rising to the wood, and lay down. A Royal Fusilier went on with the wounded man, crawling through the cover. There were left then Second Lieutenant Needham, one Royal Dublin Fusilier, and the Brigade-Major.

The Turks came up quite close, and a machine gun opened fire some forty yards away, firing obliquely under cover of the wood and making use of the depression in the ground. The party of three decided to bolt; they crawled into the wood, and did what was possible to find if there was any one left there alive, but apparently the wounded had got clear.

Both sides were now firing at the wood, and nothing could be seen of the British, every one had gone back. This had been done because the French on the extreme right had retired, and the 88th Brigade had conformed to their movement. A run for something like a mile brought shelter behind a line of South Wales Borderers, of the 87th Brigade, in response to a signal from Captain Greenway.

It took more than a month and many lives to regain the ground which was ours on this day, and all this time the Turks were digging and transforming the slopes of Krithia into outworks of the Achi Baba stronghold. But it must be remembered that the only troops available were those who had fought and lost fifty per cent. of their numbers during the three preceding days and nights.

On learning the result of the reconnaissance Major-General Marshall approved of a plan to pivot the line of the 87th and 86th on the left, and to swing round the right in order to take the entrenchments which were holding up the left.

As the troops in the centre fell back this plan could not be carried out, as there was insufficient daylight left to organize protection for the right flank. To make the best of matters before dark, orders were given to dig in on a line, later known as the Eski line. Troops which had fallen back were got into position, and a continuous line was made across the peninsula, the French joining the British by the East Krithia road. This was done during the night, which was dark and wet.

Fortunately the Turks made no counter-attack during this night of the 28th—29th April, and the day of the 29th also passed quietly. Certain re-adjustments of the line were able to be made. Barbed wire was brought up with which to construct obstacles, reserves of ammunition were collected and the position was strengthened.

When the Brigade-Major went to arrange for the consolidation of the position, only one officer of the Royal Dublin Fusiliers was left, Lieutenant O'Hara, who rose to every occasion with the greatest coolness and competence, from commanding a platoon at the terrible landing from the *River Clyde* to the command of a company the next day, and after the 28th April to commanding the battalion.

On the morning of the 30th Colonel H. G. Casson,

C.M.G., was appointed to command the brigade. About 1.10 p.m. a strong skirmishing line was observed to be advancing from the direction of Achi Baba.

The Royal Munster Fusiliers and the Royal Dublin Fusiliers were temporarily amalgamated into one unit under Major Hutchinson, and held the right of the section allotted to the brigade; the Lancashire Fusiliers were on their left, and the Royal Fusiliers entrenched in reserve. The strength of the brigade had been reduced to—

2nd Royal Fusiliers, 12 officers, 481 other ranks; 1st Lancashire Fusiliers, 11 officers, 399 other ranks; 1st Royal Munster Fusiliers, 12 officers, 596 other ranks; 1st Royal Dublin Fusiliers, 1 officer, 374 other ranks; from the normal strength per battalion of 26 officers and (approximately) 1000 other ranks.

Sniping was continuous, and late in the day the position was heavily shelled.

Brigade Headquarters had been established under shelter of the walls about a ruined stone farm-house, later known as Fig Tree Farm, close to the firing line, because it had been desirable for many reasons to be on the spot. Here were beautiful fig-trees and a garden, grown wild with flowers in bloom.

In the afternoon General Hunter-Weston visited the line and ordered Brigade Headquarters to be moved further back.

On the 1st May the day was spent in strengthening the position and resting the men. Reinforcements, stores, and guns were landed.

At dusk an action began which increased in violence as the night progressed. Somewhat early in the night a spot difficult to defend, owing to the line being pierced at an angle by bifurcating nullahs, was rushed, and a number of the enemy succeeded in breaking through. A counter-attack with the bayonet by the Royal Fusiliers and some of the Essex regiment led by Captain Pepys was successful.

All through the operations the Royal Fusiliers worked with the smoothest precision; never for a moment did they lose their high standard of efficiency. No task was relinquished while it was humanly possible to complete it. With such men as Moore, Shafto, and Hope-Johnston in control, all officers inspiring confidence, and the disciplined conduct of the men showing their friendly trust in them, there was never a fear that the reserve might fail in stemming the assault. Captain Moore, in telephonic communication throughout the night with the firing line and Brigade Headquarters, gave accurate and constant information of the progress of the fight, and acted on his own initiative or carried out orders rapidly to deal with every situation.

The firing was heavy, and, in spite of a brigade reserve of 70,000 rounds which had been accumulated by the ruined farm-house, more ammunition was needed. When the line was broken, some forty men fell back till they were stopped at Brigade Headquarters. It was a platoon which had lost its officer and accustomed N.C.O.'s.

The men were told that there was an opportunity to make up for their conduct. They jumped at the chance. Under a heavy fire, led by Captain Kane, who was temporarily acting as Staff-Captain, and the staff clerk, Sergeant Burton (lately of Messrs. Cox and Co.), they made three journeys to the firing line, carrying boxes of ammunition. No mean feat in pitch darkness, over broken country and with bullets flying, and the men were eventually allowed to resume their places in the firing line.

Later it was learnt, from copies which were found

of the Turkish orders for the attack, that this had been made by 16,000 of their best troops, with 2000 in reserve. The fiercest fighting was against the Irish regiments, who were defending the weakest part of the line and bore the greatest weight of the attack. When the masses were checked close to the British line, Germans could be heard cursing, and the sound of blows as they tried to urge on the Turks. In the morning there were dead in piles close to the British trenches. A certain number of the enemy came in and gave themselves up.

At dawn the sight was wonderful; the countryside alive with the enemy in retreat, the French artillery and our own dealing death to them with shrapnel. Many snipers were left close to the line, and the sniping on the 2nd May was very severe.

A counter-attack was ordered, but owing to the absence of adequate artillery support and the heavy fire to which our troops were subjected from the moment of showing themselves beyond the trenches, no progress was made and the line previously held was resumed. The night of the 2nd—3rd May there was an attack by the enemy, but it was not seriously pressed.

The 3rd May was quiet, and was spent by both sides in bringing in wounded and burying dead. Subsequently the Turks never permitted this. That night there was continuous firing and shelling by the enemy.

Of all brave men who throughout this period deserve most generous gratitude there is Pirie, the surgeon. He was apparently untiring. To realize the casualties is to know his task, fulfilled with sympathy, fine skill, and unruffled nerve. He ignored danger.